RISK & INNOVATION

The Role and Importance of Small High-Tech Companies in the U.S. Economy

Committee on
Technology, Management, and Capital in
Small High-Tech Companies

National Academy of Engineering

NATIONAL ACADEMY PRESS
WASHINGTON, D.C. 1995

NATIONAL ACADEMY PRESS • 2101 Constitution Avenue, NW • Washington, DC 20418

NOTICE: The National Academy of Engineering was established in 1964, under the charter of the National Academy of Sciences, as a parallel organization of outstanding engineers. It is autonomous in its administration and in the selection of its members, sharing with the National Academy of Sciences the responsibility for advising the federal government. The National Academy of Engineering also sponsors engineering programs aimed at meeting national needs, encourages education and research, and recognizes the superior achievements of engineers. Dr. Harold Liebowitz is president of the National Academy of Engineering.

This publication has been reviewed by a group other than the authors according to procedures approved by a National Academy of Engineering report review process.

Partial funding for this effort was provided by the Alfred P. Sloan Foundation.

Library of Congress Catalogue Card Number 95-72005

International Standard Book Number 0-309-05376-5

Printed in the United States of America

Preface

Small firms play a critical role in the U.S. economy. Between 1980 and 1990, U.S. employment in both manufacturing and services grew by 19 million jobs. Over the same period of time, employment in Fortune 500 companies shrank by three million jobs. During the 1970s and 1980s, new technologies, deregulation, and the destabilizing effect of imports on markets created many new niches for growth-oriented company builders. Coupled with the drastic shrinkage in many big companies' market share due to increased competition, small business began to account for a larger portion of GNP and employment. In addition to small business' increasing share of GNP and employment, these firms are also among the country's most innovative.

Small companies often have been ignored or mis-perceived during the last 15 years of debate about national competitiveness and economic globalization. Because of the critical role of small high-tech companies in the national economy the NAE, with the support of the Alfred P. Sloan Foundation, undertook the project leading to this report. The project had three major elements:

a) Six industry-specific workshops were held to explore the range and nature of critical issues facing smaller, high-technology companies, including trends in organization, technology management practices, human resource policies, government assistance initiatives, and financing. The six workshops covered the following industries: advanced displays and visual systems, network services and access devices, software, environmental testing labs, outdoor sporting goods, and medical devices. Each workshop was chaired by a member of the NAE study committee (see page iii).

b) Staff research, commissioned papers and workshop participant presentations served as the basis for a brief industry study for each of the industries examined. Those papers are published separately[1] and address the competitive parameters of the industry, areas of agreement about best practice, areas of disagreement about best practice, and areas for further investigation.

c) The study committee, working with NAE staff, prepared this report which compares and contrasts the six industries and presents findings about the role of small, high-tech companies in the U.S. economy and the role of public policy in the performance of small, high-tech companies.

On behalf of the Academy of Engineering I would like to thank the members of the study committee for their time and effort on behalf of this project. The NAE staff also deserve thanks for their work on this project, especially Bruce Guile, who directed the project, Janet Hunziker, Simon Glynn, and Vivienne Chin.

Henry Kressel
Study Chairman

---

[1]National Academy of Engineering, *Small Companies in Six Industries: Background Papers for the NAE Risk and Innovation Study* (Washington, DC: National Academy Press, forthcoming in 1996).

Contents

1

Executive Summary

INTRODUCTION

This report examines the role of small high-tech companies, including high-tech start-ups, in the development of six different industries. That examination is used:

- to draw some conclusions about the role of small companies in the development of industries and the economy;
- to characterize the industry-specific conditions that determine the opportunities for small high-tech companies; and
- to examine how government policy either limits or increases the ability of small high-tech companies to contribute to industries and the economy.

The findings and conclusions of the study are based on committee members' experiences and on insights developed by comparing and contrasting the role of small technologically innovative companies in the six industries studied: advanced displays and visual systems; implantable and surgical medical devices; software; environmental testing services; network services and access devices; and outdoor sporting goods.

Current government policies and programs are not evaluated. The committee's approach to the policy issues was to ask, How do government policies affect the formation and survival of small high-tech companies? The committee elected to focus on general policy practices and effects rather than specific programs, recognizing that government programs affecting small high-tech businesses are varied and constantly evolving.

For the purposes of this investigation, a high-tech company is one in which technical innovation or specialized technical competence is regarded as one of a limited number of key elements of competitive success. A small company is defined relative to industry norms—small companies in an industry have many established, or plausible potential, competitors that are the same size or larger in terms of employees or revenues.

THE ROLES OF TECHNOLOGICAL START-UPS AND SMALL INNOVATIVE COMPANIES IN THE U.S. ECONOMY

The industries studied for this project illustrate the technological, market, and policy risks often borne by small companies. They also illustrate how a varied set of small companies pioneer and develop new markets and provide product diversity and innovation in small markets.

Small companies in the software and the network devices and services industries are prototypically entrepreneurial and high-tech. New company formation is supported by: relative ease of entry because of relatively low initial capital requirements; a significant number of successes, which serve to encourage entrepreneurs to enter the industry; companies that appear to have substantial value if sold, even though they are not necessarily long-term survivors; availability of venture capital financing; and a public market for the shares of companies at relatively high valuations, compared with other industries, on the basis of revenues or profitability. In both of these industries, there are large, dominant companies, but the technological dynamism and fragmentation of the market create opportunities for small companies. In both software and network industries, the development and commercial proof of a wide range of emerging technologies, as well as the development and growth of the industry, depend on the investments and actions of small companies willing to take linked technological and business risks.

Small companies play an unusual role in the advanced display industry. In the early 1990s, technological uncertainty, widely expected but unrealized large markets, and government (Department of Defense) funding created a cadre of small, relatively research-intensive companies in search of a valuable proprietary technological position. In the advanced display industry, small companies have been the repository of technical capability during the development of both core and complementary technologies and products.

In both the outdoor sporting goods and implantable and surgical medical device industries, user-inventors play an important role in bringing new products to market. Also, in both industries, small companies and user-inventors have provided innovation and product diversity in small markets (i.e., markets that are too small to attract and hold the attention of larger innovative companies). Differences are also evident.

In medical device innovation, most user-inventors are highly technically trained, the "field testing" of products is often a formal clinical trial in a university hospital, and, historically, venture capital was widely available for medical device start-ups. Furthermore, medical devices are sold to physicians (and increasingly to health care organizations) rather than to consumers directly, and they are increasingly regulated by the FDA, a change that industry observers believe may alter forever the way medical device innovation is done and, perhaps, eliminate small-company participation. The outdoor sporting goods industry and the implantable and surgical medical device industry illustrate the range of small markets that are served by small innovation-oriented companies. They also illustrate how small companies often pull fundamental technical advances from outside the industry into new applications.

The environmental testing service industry is dominated by small companies, but it has a unique characteristic: Demand for services is created by regulation and driven by enforcement. Barriers to entry into the industry are low, but so are the opportunities for growth; economies of scale, if they exist at all, are small, and the opportunities for innovation are slight. However, environmental testing laboratories serve an important public function. Without good testing services, environmental regulation and some aspects of environmental protection would not be possible. In this sense, environmental testing laboratories serve the economy by providing an important technical service in small, often geographically differentiated markets.

In many industries, small high-tech companies play a critical and diverse role in creating new products and services, in developing industries, and in driving technological change and growth in the U.S. economy. In consumer markets, substantial benefits of linked commercial and technological risk taking accrue directly and immediately to individual consumers and to the national economy. These benefits include the rapid exploration of market potentials, the development and refinement of new products and services, certain types of technical innovation, and product diversity. In intermediate or industrial markets, the willingness of small companies to shoulder technological and related market risks may enable other companies (both large and small) to pursue otherwise unavailable technological approaches to improving productivity or introducing new products. In small consumer and intermediate markets—slowly growing markets with total annual demand in the tens of millions rather than hundreds of millions of dollars—small companies are often the only source of products or services and are, therefore, responsible for all product diversity and for bringing innovations to the market.

These market functions are an important part of economic development and, as such, are key in the economy's learning process about which technologies, at what price, will or will not satisfy demand. The principal economic function of small, entrepreneurial, high-tech companies is to probe, explore, and sometimes develop the frontiers of the U.S. economy—in products, services, technologies, and markets—in search of unrecognized or otherwise ignored opportunities for economic growth and development.

OPPORTUNITIES FOR SMALL TECHNOLOGY-ORIENTED COMPANIES

Small technology-oriented companies exist in most industries, but they exist in abundance in industries that share the following characteristics:

• Markets that are fragmented, technically dynamic, and rapidly growing;
• Low barriers to entry;

- An adequate regional and national technical and business infrastructure;
- Good access to potential customers;
- Availability of financing; and
- A culture (recent history) of entrepreneurship in the industry.

Where these conditions exist, they are often accompanied by a predictable set of business and technological risks. The characteristics of a product or service market are key determinants of small-business technological opportunity. The demands of successful commercial innovation in different markets differ, leading to varied levels of expenditures on research, development, demonstration, and to variation in the organization of company technical effort.

Small companies can have inherent advantages in fragmented, technically dynamic, and rapidly growing markets in which there are low barriers to entry. The rapid pace of change in such business environments often creates nascent or rapidly growing markets where a small company may establish an early position by luck or skill.

The interactions between new technology-intensive companies and larger companies are myriad, diverse, and critical to the growth of many industries. Small companies can exploit certain opportunities, but that set of opportunities is often at least partially determined by the actions of larger companies. Most small companies do little research. The importance of spin-outs of technology, personnel, and business opportunities from large-company expenditures and efforts in research and development should not be underestimated as a source of opportunity for small companies.

Much high-tech activity by small companies is regionally reinforcing. The ability of some regional economies to spawn new businesses is well recognized. There are important regional sources of entrepreneurs and ideas, certain regional conditions that have an important impact on the ability of a region to foster start-ups, and a related but separate set of conditions that affect the ability of a company to grow in a region. Furthermore, there is increasing awareness of both the predictable and unpredictable dynamic characteristics of regional, high-tech economic growth. In sum, the regional vigor of entrepreneurial activity is determined in large measure by local and regional characteristics, including:

- sources of people and ideas, such as research universities and large corporate labs;
- supportive infrastructure, such as business incubators, seed capital, entrepreneurial networks, and advisory services; and
- resources for company formation and growth, such as a strong technical and managerial workforce.

HOW GOVERNMENTS CAN NURTURE SMALL COMPANIES AND TECHNOLOGICAL INNOVATORS

This study did not specifically evaluate the numerous government programs that support small high-tech businesses, but it did review programs aimed at helping small business, fostering technology development, and assisting companies that are both small and technology intensive. A number of national policy matters affect directly the prosperity and performance of small high-tech businesses. It is the committee's judgment that the federal government can help maintain the vigor and contribution of small high-tech businesses in the following ways:

- Working to ensure that financial market regulation, banking laws, and securities regulatory agencies are sensitive to the particular demands of small high-tech companies;
- Monitoring and when possible reducing federal, state, and local regulatory burdens on small high-tech companies; and
- Maintaining, especially in light of prospective cutbacks in research and development spending, a rich portfolio of university research as a source of potential new commercial opportunities for start-up companies.

A wide variety of government actions aimed at and justified by other missions—public safety, environmental quality, and national defense, for example—also have an enormous impact on small technology-intensive companies by affecting the cost of innovation or the risk of failure. The relevant question for policymakers is, What types of policies substantially encourage (reduce the risk of, or increase the likely return on) commercial technical experimentation by small companies and start-ups?

With regard to the inadvertent impact of government actions, it is clear that government itself is a substantial source of risk for some small companies; part of the risk that small high-tech businesses often bear is that created by the unintended consequences of government actions. In the committee's judgment, the consequences of government actions for technically oriented start-ups and small companies—and by implication for their ability to assume technological risk and drive innovation—are often poorly understood both by the public and by policymakers.

The committee suggests that federal activism on behalf of small business and technology initiatives focus first on establishing mechanisms within government—many of them off-budget—that can improve the general environment for innovative enterprises. Because the structure and implementation of regulations affect the character and speed of innovation (through the risks they can create or remove for companies), regulatory approaches across a wide variety of government functions need to be carefully considered with regard to their impact on small high-tech companies.

With regard to programs for active support of small technically oriented businesses, the committee suggests that the central issue is whether federal support will make a difference in the economy's technological development. Private investment is likely to be much greater than any reasonable level of public investment in fragmented, technically dynamic industries with low barriers to entry and a history of (or widely perceived prospect of) successful entrepreneurship. In such industries, the important question is, How can government research, development, and demonstration complement the much larger private investment (risk taking) to the benefit of the national economy? The challenge in program design and implementation is to articulate and adhere to an industry-specific rationale for government support in light of substantial private-sector activity.

Finally, in the committee's judgment, many government policy mechanisms to promote economic growth—some types of federal R&D funding, technical assistance programs, local business incubators, university-industry collaborative ventures—need to be designed and managed regionally or locally. Local and regional programs may have an advantage in that they are closer to the resources that small companies need and are potentially more able to adapt to the needs of small high-tech companies.

2

Introduction

It is widely understood that national economic growth and commercial technological advance are closely coupled. Technological advances as diverse as the airplane, the microprocessor, and bioengineered pharmaceuticals have increased productivity and restructured the economy in dramatic ways. While hindsight makes it possible to see the enormous economic impact of technological advances, the drivers and mechanisms of such advances are less clearly perceived. The mythology of invention and innovation gives us many possible explanations—the U.S. economy is driven by individual inventors working in their basements, by research universities, by large industrial research laboratories, by spin-offs from publicly funded defense-related research, and by small high-tech companies. This study examines the last of these commonly discussed causative factors by considering the role of small high-tech companies, including high-tech start-ups, in the development of industries and the economy. The first step in understanding the role of such companies is to characterize, at least briefly, where small companies fit in the U.S. economy.

The corporate organization of U.S. economic activity is complex and highly varied. At the top end of the size spectrum, the combined 1994 annual sales of the 10 largest U.S. industrial companies was approximately $700 billion, or an average of $70 billion per company. All those companies are publicly traded. There are approximately 8,000 publicly traded companies in the United States[1] and about 12,000 companies with annual revenues over $50 million. These two sets of companies overlap but not entirely. In addition there are about 60,000 companies with annual revenues between $50 and $10 million, almost 500,000 businesses with annual revenues less than $10 million but over $1 million, and approximately 17 million tax-filing businesses with annual revenues of less than $1 million.[2]

It is difficult to get a comprehensive perspective on such business complexity. If the *Wall Street Journal* dedicated one column-inch—about 60 words—to every U.S. company with annual revenues over $10 million, the issue would run about 600 pages. Small or rapidly growing high-tech companies, however, get quite a bit of attention both in the media and in policy circles. The media focus on dramatic stories of success, savvy, folly, and failure. Investors, would-be entrepreneurs, and business managers read and learn something about what worked and did not work for certain companies. Policymakers, and their economic advisers, focus on the contribution of high-tech companies to the creation of jobs and to national technological prowess. This report focuses on the role of such business organizations in the growth and development of particular industries and of the economy as a whole.

THE STUDY APPROACH

The study leading to this report was conducted between mid-1993 and early-1995. The purposes of the study were

• to draw some general conclusions about the role of small companies in the development of industries and the economy;

• to characterize the industry-specific economic conditions which determine the opportunities for small high-tech companies; and

---

[1]Nasdaq Backgrounder: The NASDAQ Stock Market (Washington, D.C.: NASDAQ, 1995).

[2]R. Crawford and W. Sihler, The Troubled Money Business (New York: Harper Business, 1991).

- to examine how the intent and implementation of government policy either limits or increases the ability of small high-tech companies to contribute to the development of industries and the economy.

The findings and conclusions of the study are based, in part, on committee member's experiences (see committee list, p. iii). To broaden the base of consideration beyond the experience of the study committee, the study also examined six industries in which small high-tech companies play a significant role:

Advanced displays and visual systems. Advanced displays include several competing flat panel display technologies and also projection systems and video presentation equipment used in advanced electronics systems, such as full-color notebook computers or aircraft display systems.

Implantable and surgical medical devices. Implantable and surgical devices are designed for implantation in the human body, such as shoulder prostheses and left ventricular assist devices, or for manipulating human organs and tissues, especially devices used to perform minimally invasive therapy. These devices include angioplasty catheters, endoscopes, and a variety of accessory device technologies, including lasers and miniaturized forceps.

Software. Software is ubiquitous. For the purposes of this study, software products can be somewhat artificially divided into (a) prepackaged software, for example, database or word processing applications and (b) customized "enterprise" software and services, including systems integration to help clients address specific requirements.

Environmental testing services. Environmental testing laboratories perform assessments for industry and government agencies regarding the nature and extent of environmental contamination in water, soil, air, and waste products.

Network services and access devices. Rapid growth in the nation's general-purpose communications assets (phone lines, satellites, cellular systems) has combined with growth of distributed computer processing and the refinement of input devices (readers, sensors, etc.) to create a host of new "network" services.

Outdoor sporting goods. Outdoor sporting goods, as defined for this study, include such items as technical outerwear, climbing ropes and gear, kayaks and canoes, in-line skates, special-purpose hand tools, hand-held global positioning devices, and "mountain" bicycles.

In addition to staff research, the study committee organized and held six sector-specific workshops, drawing heavily on small-business entrepreneurs from the industry. Brief industry studies, based in part on these workshops and focused on the role of small companies, are published separately.[3] No study that relies on a small committee and a small sample of industries can be exhaustive; the roles of small high-tech companies in an industry and the characteristics of successful small companies in an industry vary to a degree that few generalizations apply. Within the scope of the present study, the purpose of comparing and contrasting these industries was to identify and understand the different roles that small high-tech companies play in selected industries and the economy as a whole, and to extract lessons for small high-tech company success and, by implication, for government policy.

DEFINITIONS AND POLICY QUESTIONS

Three final introductory notes are useful to define what this report means by "high-tech" and by "small," and to discuss briefly the nature of the public policy challenges addressed in this study.

With regard to the definition of "high-tech," this study relies more on an assessment of industry dynamics than on measures of technical expenditures or assets employed. Traditionally, high-tech companies are defined as those companies (a) that spend a relatively high proportion of annual revenue on R&D or (b) that employ a relatively high proportion of scientists and engineers in

---

[3]National Academy of Engineering, *Small Companies in Six Industries: Background Papers for the NAE Risk and Innovation Study* (Washington, D.C.: National Academy Press, forthcoming in 1996).

their total workforce.[4] By these criteria a three-person, R&D-oriented start-up in the garage of a university engineering professor, with no sales and no manufacturing, is a model high-tech company. Although these firms are important they represent a narrow segment of companies this report considers. **For the purposes of this investigation, therefore, a high-tech company is one in which technical innovation or specialized technical competence is regarded as one of a limited number of key elements of competitive success.**

This definition expands the universe of high-tech companies to include those that do no formal R&D, but compete on the basis of applications of technology. For example, in the high-end of outdoor sporting apparel or bicycle manufacture, there is fierce competition over certain technically determined product characteristics. The materials advances may be driven by R&D in large, integrated manufacturers of textiles, metals, or composites, but the small companies who design, manufacture, test, and market the products in a technologically dynamic marketplace—often with no R&D budget and relatively few technical professionals—are treated by this study as high-tech companies.

On the matter of company size, although there are quantitative measures such as annual revenues or number of employees for characterizing small companies, these numbers are ultimately not very satisfying. For example, using typical definitions of small as set by the Small Business Administration (under 500 employees—see the Appendix for discussion of definitions) and used in the majority of empirical analyses, a 450-employee, publicly traded, $70 million medical device company that is dominant in its market is considered small. **For the purposes of this investigation, small is determined relative to industry sector norms. In general, small companies in an industry have many established, or plausible potential, competitors that are the same size (employees or revenues) or larger.**

---

[4]For example, *Science and Engineering Indicators*, the annual databook produced by the U.S. National Science Board, draws data from a variety of sources, most of which rely on a ratio of R&D expenditures (however defined) to shipments to determine which companies or products are high-tech. National Science Board, Science & Engineering Indicators (Washington, D.C.: National Science Board, 1993).

With regard to policy issues, while the study committee reviewed the full range of government programs aimed at small and high-tech businesses, no attempt was made to evaluate specific programs. **The focus of this investigation has been the conditions under which small high-tech companies thrive. The approach to the policy arguments included here has been in asking the question, How do government policies affect the likelihood of small high-tech company formation and survival?**

The committee elected to focus on general policy practices and effects rather than specific programs, recognizing that government programs affecting small high-tech businesses are varied and constantly evolving. The following significant events have occurred since the start of this study:

- A major Department of Defense program to provide support for the advanced display industry has been initiated.
- The rapid ramp up of technology-oriented programs with implications for small businesses—especially the Advanced Technology Program (ATP) in the National Institute of Standards and Technology, and the Technology Reinvestment Program (TRP) in the Department of Defense—followed shortly by strong moves toward rapid reduction in these programs under the Congress elected in the fall of 1994.
- Apparently real and significant threats to current levels of Department of Defense (DOD)-sponsored academic research funding as the end of the Cold War brings a re-evaluation of DOD research and development priorities.
- The issuance of a draft Federal Accounting Standards Board (FASB) rule on the ways in which stock options are carried on a company's books, followed by the withdrawal of the rule as a result of a firestorm of criticism from the entrepreneurial, high-tech community.
- The announcement of new legislation, brought forward as part of the Republican "Contract with America" to limit product liability and, significantly for small high-tech companies, to limit the exposure of companies to stock fraud suits on the basis of substantial fluctuations in stock price.
- The presentation of seriously received federal budget proposals from the House and the Senate that include, among other actions, cuts in the Small Business Administration as well as in

programs of the National Institute of Standards and Technology such as ATP (already noted) and those for the support of manufacturing extension services.

In short, the policy environment for small high-tech companies continues to change rapidly. This study's contribution to policy is to advance understanding of the principles that should distinguish good policy and programs from bad rather than attempting an evaluation of current or currently proposed programs and policies.

THE STRUCTURE OF THE REPORT

This report is divided into three major sections. The next chapter—The Roles of Technological Start-Ups and Small Innovative Companies in the U.S. Economy—focuses on the six sectors described above. For each sector, the chapter identifies the explicit and implicit expectations of small companies in the development of the sector and of technologies employed in the industry. These analyses are then followed by the committee's assessment of the principal economic role of small companies, as well as a distillation of the divergent set of issues that appear to affect the role of small technically oriented companies. The chapter on Opportunities for Small Technology-Oriented Companies examines the ways in which certain characteristics of industries, regions, and technologies affect the attractiveness of business opportunities for small technologically innovative companies. The primary contribution of this chapter is the identification and description of those market and technological characteristics that create a large number of opportunities for small high-tech companies. The final chapter provides an overview of current government policies, and the effects of these policies on the opportunities for small technology-intensive companies.

3

The Roles of Technological Start-Ups and Small Innovative Companies in the U.S. Economy

Commercial innovation is inherently risky. To the normal business risks, technical innovators add the risks of technical failure or failure to match a technological advance with a market demand. In certain types of commercial technological advance, exploration by small firms is a critical part of the learning process of the industry. This is not a new phenomenon. In the early days of the automobile industry, for example, the development of technology and *de facto* industry standards were driven by small technological risk-takers. Between 1895 and 1923 the number of automobile manufacturers grew from 0 to 75. In 1923 Dodge introduced the all-steel, closed-body automobile and the number of companies dropped precipitously as this new industry standard (and a much smaller number of companies) grew to capture 80 percent of the market by 1926. The scale advantages in production were reflected in sharply lower costs, and by the early 1930s the number of automobile manufacturers had dropped to 25.[1] Historical distance allows us to see this pattern clearly, a pattern that future historians

---

[1]J.M. Utterback, Innovation and industrial evolution in manufacturing industries. Pp. 16-48 in *Technology and Global Industry*, B. Guile and H. Brooks, eds. (Washington, D.C.: National Academy Press, 1987).

of industrial technical change are likely to be able to identify in personal computers, software, and biotechnology.

Indeed, the biotechnology industry represents a particularly dramatic contemporaneous example of the phenomenon. The formation of this new industry was catalyzed by advances in fundamental biology in the 1960s and 1970s, and in particular, by the invention of technology that provided the capability of synthesizing complex natural proteins, such as human insulin, by inserting the requisite gene into simple microorganisms. The rate of formation of new firms dedicated to the exploitation of one or another aspect of this new technology has been phenomenal; approximately 800 new enterprises were founded in the decade of the 1980s, and the industry currently numbers more than 1,200 firms. A few of these firms have become large, successful operating companies (e.g., Amgen), but the vast majority of biotech firms are small investor-funded R&D ventures.

The biotechnology industry has demonstrated itself to be an effective vehicle for rapid societal exploration of the potential of a set of powerful new technologies. However, it appears that the associated high risks were somewhat obscured by a few dramatic early successes achieved by the pioneer firms. Most recently, the spectacular advances in biotechnology have become qualified by the high costs for a course of therapy that uses the new drugs, reflecting the high spending by biotechnology companies to develop these new drugs. A recent spate of failures of prospective biotech medicines in clinical trials, coupled with the emergence of a more difficult market for costly health care products, has made raising capital extremely difficult for all but the best-positioned biotech firms. A closed financial market, if long continued, could lead to a substantially restructured industry, and perhaps the closing of this "exploratory" phase of biotech commercialization.

These demands of pioneering new markets—of driving such societal technological learning—change dramatically in short periods of time as a function of changes in technology, market demand, and industry maturity. Table 1 names a few of the typical factors increasing and decreasing risk borne by companies, of all sizes, engaged in technology-dependent ventures. Some of these risk factors are best negotiated by larger companies—they may be better equipped to minimize the risk or survive an adverse outcome—but some are successfully tolerated or managed only by

TABLE 1   Factors that Increase and Decrease Risk Associated with Technology Investments

Factors Increasing Risk	Factors Decreasing Risk
Totally new market or low experience in the market with the product or service	Expansion in existing market
Strong competitors	No dominant competitors
Technological uncertainty	Government technology funding or steps to create the market by purchases
Environmental uncertainty	Stable standards—environmental, technological, social, etc.
High potential product liability (medical products, nuclear, toxics, etc.)	Relevant government infrastructure
Changing industry standards	External investment partners with large resources (cooperative venture)
Marginal internal skills— not "leading edge"	"Safe harbors" from product liability for certain products (vaccines, defense products, etc.)
Restricted market access, especially in worldwide markets	Guaranteed access to foreign or government technology or other external sources
Little protection for intellectual property	Strong patent or copyright protection
Regulatory barriers to commercialization	

small companies. Small companies may systematically face a different risk/reward line than larger companies; some risks may be differentially critical to small companies.

For example, small suppliers to large companies may have to commit the bulk of their company's resources to satisfy the demands of a single buyer. For such a small company, the consequence of a change in plans or purchasing by its primary customer, or of a failure on the part of the small company to deliver quality product, could easily be bankruptcy. Another example is a policy or regulatory change that lengthens the time to market for a new product being brought out by a start-up company. The costs of keeping the company solvent during the lengthened period between development expenditures and positive cash flow may be too much for a thinly capitalized small company. In a larger company, it is much more likely that the resources will be available to tolerate a delay.

COMPARING THE CONTRIBUTIONS OF SMALL TECHNOLOGY-ORIENTED COMPANIES

The technological risks of commercial companies are different than those of non-market research and development. In addition to the risk that a new technology may not work as expected, there is the competitive market risk: can a product or service using a new technology deliver adequate value for its price in comparison with competing offerings? In general, to reduce real and persistent technical and market uncertainties, the bulk of small technically oriented companies and start-ups tend to focus on *incremental* market-driven innovations, and not breakthrough technologies; small company innovation often reflects the shape of perceived market opportunity. Based on the industries studied for this project, it is clear that small companies are often compelled to focus on incremental, market-driven innovation by the immediate, and at times overwhelming, risk of running out of money.

Further, the limitations of small companies' abilities to reduce technical and market uncertainty constrain the character of new opportunities and drive dependence on outside technical resources. For most small companies the opportunities for incremental commercial innovation are shaped by advances in science and technology from outside the company—usually in universities or large company research laboratories; often entrepreneurs are intimately familiar with these advances, either as they were directly involved or know well the people doing the research. The ability of small companies to develop, in-house, advances in science and technology that create new opportunities is usually restricted to a relatively narrow scope, reflecting the expertise of the technical members of the small company, as well as their previous experience.

Government policies also shape the opportunities and the level of risk for small companies, both directly and indirectly. Direct government funding—research grants and government mission-oriented R&D contracts—can reduce the risks of technology commercialization for small companies. These types of support are most important for emerging technologies that have not yet been proven to be commercially viable. Much more frequently, however, government policies shape the opportunities for small companies indirectly. In particular, small high-tech companies tend to be relatively vulnerable to risk created by the legal system and by government policies such as health and safety regulations, employment and environmental regulations, and export controls.

The industries studied for this project illustrate the types of technological and policy risk borne by a representative group of small companies. Most important, they illustrate how small companies pioneer and develop new markets and provide product diversity and innovation in small markets.[2]

Advanced Displays and Visual Systems

Although cathode ray tube (CRT) technology continues to dominate electronic displays, large and expanding opportunities exist where the CRT's power requirements and physical dimensions cannot be accommodated, and alternative display technologies must be used. These technologies include increasingly ubiqui-

---

[2]The brief industry descriptions provided in this chapter are drawn from the longer industry studies prepared as part of the study project. The estimates of typical or average company size, market sizes, and market growth rates in each of the industry descriptions are drawn from an unusually diverse set of published resources, most often the industry's trade literature or material prepared by the industry's trade association. The arguments about industry structure and dynamics were developed during the industry-specific workshops held for this study or drawn from trade and industry association publications. The sources for these generally reliable but less-than-perfect numbers and arguments are provided in the separately published industry studies. National Academy of Engineering, *Small Companies in Six Industries: Background Papers for the NAE Risk and Innovation Study* (Washington, D.C.: National Academy Press, forthcoming in 1996).

tous flat panel displays, already used in full-color notebook computers, aircraft avionics, and a variety of handheld computer games and electronic devices, as well as new display technologies that typically involve projection for presentation systems and wide-screen high-definition televisions. These advanced displays are expected to be among the most critical and perhaps expensive components of the next generation of these devices. For example, the market for just flat panel displays is expected to triple by 2000, from $3.7 billion in 1993.

Advanced displays and visual systems are unique in the sectors studied for this project, in two respects. First, Japan dominates advanced displays, not the United States. In 1992 Japanese companies produced 98 percent of the world supply of flat panel displays, and essentially built all screens using active-matrix liquid crystal display (LCD) technology. Competition among the major Japanese companies has accelerated Japanese investment in this technology to more than $3 billion by 1993, effectively making LCD the dominant advanced display technology for the foreseeable future. This is in contrast to the situation that has evolved in the United States, where there has been an almost complete absence of large investments in active matrix LCD production to date.

The second respect in which advanced displays and visual systems are different from the other sectors in this project is in the relatively few U.S. companies that compete in advanced displays. In contrast to Japan, efforts to commercialize advanced displays in the United States over the last decade have been largely by a group of 10 to 20 small, technology-intensive companies pursuing a variety of next-generation technologies. Many of these are spin-offs from the R&D efforts of larger, technology-based U.S. companies that exited the advanced display market in the 1980s.

The reason these small companies exist in advanced displays is that, with few exceptions, the market pull for the next generation of display technologies is undeveloped in many potential applications. For example, plasma and electro-luminescence technologies compete with LCDs, as well as with several other emerging technologies (e.g., field emission displays, microtip displays, vacuum-fluorescent displays). But no one technology has yet emerged that is able to meet the requirements (e.g., cost, power consumption, image contrast, color, manufacturability) for all applications. This creates enormous technological uncertainty that centers on a few, critical questions: How well will the new technologies perform? How expensive will these technologies be to develop and produce in volume? Will these new technologies be able to eclipse current LCD technologies that are likely to continue to improve?

In response to this uncertainty, small U.S. companies have exploited opportunities to develop different technologies for different applications. In this respect, they do not conduct research per se; rather they focus on technically challenging product development and engineering. Few if any companies have grown solely from technological or scientific breakthroughs. The most successful small companies have identified a market need and adapted existing technology to fill that need.

Federal technology policies, in particular support from the Advanced Research Projects Agency of the Department of Defense, have also been critical to developing these technologies by creating a degree of stability in the opportunities for small U.S. display companies, typically by awards directly to small companies in the form of grants or development contracts from the Department of Defense.

More recently, mergers and partnerships between these small entrepreneurial companies and larger companies have also become increasingly frequent, for several reasons. As opportunities for advanced displays have been proven (primarily by Japanese competitors), larger U.S. electronics companies have realized (a) the large current and potential markets for the right new technology, (b) the value of in-house capability in components as fundamental as displays, and (c) the risks of not being current in display product and production technology.

Small R&D-intensive companies are increasingly aware that the challenges and cost of scale-up from prototype to production effectively limit their ability to push technology. First among these challenges is obtaining sufficient capital. This is especially true of LCDs for which a single factory to produce displays in volume can cost between $100 million and $300 million. In addition to capital, there are a number of serious technical challenges associated with the manufacture of displays. For example, a lack of standardized process equipment greatly complicates display manufacturing. The United States has also lacked a robust display infrastructure in which to develop, test, and sell equipment. The supply of properly trained scientists and engineers has also been small.

In summary, small companies in advanced displays play an unusual role. The demand for advanced displays is expected to be very large, but many of the markets are (as yet) unrealized, creating enormous uncertainty about the next generation of display technologies. This technological uncertainty—and therefore risk—as well as direct government support of advanced displays technologies has created a cadre of small, relatively research-intensive companies in search of a valuable proprietary technological position. These companies represent, in effect, a repository of technical capability in advanced displays. But the capital requirements for scale-up and the technological issues of manufacturing for large markets—including the relatively weak infrastructure in the United States for advanced displays—severely limit the opportunities for small companies to exploit these technological advances. Indeed, they will increasingly be compelled to form partnerships with larger companies or be acquired, as core and complementary technologies in displays advance.

Implantable and Surgical Medical Devices

The U.S. market for medical devices and dental equipment is estimated at around $40 billion. This significant aggregate figure, however, conceals a fragmented market including on the order of 1,700 different types of medical devices.

The term "implantable and surgical" refers to the subset of medical devices intended for implantation in the human body, such as shoulder prostheses and left ventricular assist devices, or for manipulating human organs and tissues, especially devices used to perform minimally invasive therapy. Some of the more important devices include angioplasty catheters, endoscopes, and a variety of accessory device technologies including lasers and miniaturized forceps. The size of the market opportunities for these high-tech devices tends to be relatively modest, ranging from tens to hundreds of millions of dollars per year in the United States. Within vascular surgery, for example, the size of the market in 1991 ranged from less than $10 million for vascular probes, to about $30 million for carotid shunts, to about $70 million for vascular grafts.

Technological innovation in these niche-markets depends critically on this risk-taking by entrepreneurial individuals and small companies. In contrast, larger companies may not have the ability or patience to develop innovations for small markets—the risk is too high and the return too low. The economics of device research, development, and demonstration can make these markets unattractive to larger companies until the application of technology is well proven in the market. The fragmentation in these markets is reflected in the relatively large number of small companies that are involved in medical devices—between 10,000 and 11,000 device firms, either domestic or foreign, operate in the United States. Of these, more than 70 percent of U.S. medical device manufacturers have fewer than 50 employees.

Universities are important to medical device innovation in the United States. First, universities and academic medical centers tend to be the locus for innovation in medical devices, as well as for the development of new devices. Frequently, medical device innovation is driven by what can best be characterized as "hobby shop" innovation by highly trained specialists in universities or academic medical centers. In particular, devices used in limited quantities—such as specialized stents used to hold open clogged vessels—are often designed and developed (at least initially) by individual surgeons or physicians who, as part of their academic or clinical work, see a better way of doing something and work with a small team to create a new device or paired device and procedure.

Universities are especially important in another sense. In contrast to pharmaceutical development, innovation in implantable and surgical medical devices tends to look far outside the realm of biomedical research for new technological opportunities. Medical device innovation results largely from incremental, engineering-based innovation that transfers new technologies into medicine. Innovations in imaging technologies are an example of this. The computerized tomographic (CT) scanner or magnetic resonance imager (MRI), for example, depended on the transfer into medicine of advances in other areas, including mathematics and computers, electronics, optics, and material sciences. Equally, much of the technological dynamism of current developments of the endoscope use semiconductor chips for imaging, as well as fiber-optic technologies. Universities and academic medical centers are especially important as the locus of this technology transfer.

Government policies also have a powerful impact on medical device innovation. First, the government is a major source of medical R&D funding. Second, the Food and Drug Administration

(FDA) influences the selection and development of new medical devices through its premarketing approval and regulations for medical devices. Third, the government, primarily through the growth of Medicare, has become a major source of payment to the providers of medical services. Consequently, government decisions about what to pay for, and how much to pay, are an important influence on the incentives for small company risk taking.

Currently, radical changes in this regulatory and policy environment for medical devices are raising questions about the viability of the innovative enterprise which has driven linked technical and therapeutic advances in smaller segments of the medical device industry. First, more stringent FDA regulation of medical devices requiring increased numbers of trials and evaluation increases the expected time to market of new devices and increases the cost of demonstrating new devices, increasing the business risk. This translates directly into a more difficult financial environment for device start-ups.

Second, a serious effort continues toward radical reform of the health care financing and delivery system through legislation. These reform efforts and changing reimbursement policies also increase the uncertainty with regard to device markets and consequently the risk. Increased sensitivity to the cost of medical care has also changed the model for adoption and use of new medical devices. Previously, adoption in medical devices depended on an intimate model of evaluation and dissemination of new medical devices by colleagues of the inventor and other physicians; adoption decisions were not particularly sensitive to cost. By contrast, a different model is now emerging as payers—health care insurers and federal agencies—increasingly restrict, through decisions affecting cost coverage, the adoption of new technologies by individual physicians. These changes may have vast implications for innovation and for the viability of small companies in medical devices.

To summarize, small companies and entrepreneurs are exceedingly important for innovation in medical devices. The high degree of regulation in medical devices, as well as recent changes in this regulation, affects the economics and direction of medical device R&D, creating a high degree of economic risk. This risk, as well as the large technological risks and relatively fragmented markets for medical devices, makes these opportunities unattractive to larger companies until the technology and application have been demonstrated. For these reasons, medical device innovation and product diversity appear to depend, perhaps to a surprising extent, on individual user-inventors. In an academic or clinical setting—usually a university or academic medical center—these user-investors transfer technologies developed in other areas and for other uses into medicine and in that way create new medical devices.

Software

While the roots of the software industry are firmly planted in the early history of commercial mainframe computers, the current software industry—largely unbundled from hardware and dominated by applications running on personal computers, workstations, and networks—did not exist as recently as 15 years ago. In economic terms, the majority of software development continues to be done internally by companies—spending for maintenance and incremental improvement to existing software is estimated to be as high as $150 billion to $200 billion. But spending for new software is increasingly used to buy either prepackaged software or customized software and services. This spending for new software and services is estimated to exceed $100 billion worldwide.

Despite the increasing number of large software companies, this high level of spending for new software continues to create an extraordinary number of start-ups and small software companies. Indeed, in 1987 more than half of all U.S. software companies had fewer than five employees, 97 percent had fewer than a hundred employees, and this level of concentration in software has *declined* in the last decade.

Small companies thrive in the software industry, primarily because of two trends: (a) the rapid pace of change in electronics and software technologies, and (b) the high degree of fragmentation in markets as electronics and software seep into almost every aspect of the economy. In other words, despite its large economic size, demand for software in established applications (those a few years old) continues to increase even as technological advances and human inventiveness create new market opportunities such as multimedia.

This fragmented, rapidly growing marketplace is an ideal environment for start-ups that exploit technologies or markets deemed to be too small or too risky for established players. Thus, new markets and narrow, niche markets that lead to considerably larger markets let new software companies develop the revenue stream, product, and core competencies of valuable new software businesses.

The nature of software development also means that initial barriers to entry are extremely low—although in prepackaged software the costs and the distribution problems of selling into high-volume markets are increasing the capital requirements for new entrants. Nor do there appear to be many economies of scale in developing these applications. Indeed, the imperatives of creativity and flexibility in software development appear to favor innovative, new competitors seeking to serve limited or specialized markets. These dynamics make the investment risk-reward equation for many untested opportunities too demanding for large software companies. Instead, larger companies usually commercialize new technologies and enter new markets by acquiring a smaller company or start-up that has demonstrated success. This mechanism creates both substantial industry growth and opportunities for entrepreneurs to reap returns on their investments.

This economic organization of the software industry has consequences for the viability of new software companies. New companies may identify new markets or new technologies, but they are extremely dependent on external sources for access to capital, markets—and crucially, for distribution—management expertise. They also quickly become vulnerable to new companies with a better idea. As a result, software companies tend to be divided into three groups. The first group consists of the few companies that become large and develop the internal resources to have long-term staying power. Examples are Microsoft and Lotus.

But these are exceptions. The overwhelming majority of start-ups in software are in the second group, which develops niche-market products and reaches revenues in the $5 million to $15 million range. The life cycle of these companies is short relative to older industries—typically they will either fail when their product life cycle has run its course or be acquired by or merged with other companies to reach sustaining capabilities. The third group includes those software companies that for a variety of reasons are not successful, and fail.

Finally, in software, uncertainty over the definition and protection of intellectual property rights also has an important impact on the opportunities for small companies. Patents are expensive to obtain and are difficult to enforce and defend. In this sense, the economics of litigation favor larger companies at the expense of smaller ones. There is also ambiguity about what is and is not patentable. These ambiguities also increase risk by increasing the costs and uncertainties of litigation.

Small companies in software, then, represent in a nearly ideal form the entrepreneurial, technology-intensive start-up. Although the number of large competitors in software is increasing, the rapid development of new technologies and enormous number of new potential markets create a broad array of opportunities for technically capable small companies. The range and number of opportunities, low barriers to entry, and absence of significant economies of scale in the development of many new specialized software products favor innovative, new companies. Indeed, to a considerable extent, development and commercial proof of emerging technologies and markets in software depend on the investments and actions of small companies willing to accept technological (and financial) risk.

Environmental Testing Services

The roots of the environmental testing industry can be traced back to 1962, when drinking water standards advanced by the U.S. Public Health Service spurred the development of water quality testing labs. This nascent industry consisted of small in-house water utility labs, as well as commercial "mom and pop" laboratories that tested for a variety of simple parameters such as water hardness, some metals, and coliform bacteria. Industry growth accelerated with the introduction of the first two major pieces of environmental legislation requiring extensive analytical testing— the Federal Water Pollution Control Act amendments of 1972 (now referred to as the Clean Water Act, or CWA), and the Safe Drinking Water Act of 1974 (SDWA).

A second wave of major environmental legislation increased the demand for commercial environmental laboratory services exponentially starting in the late 1970s and early 1980s. The two seminal pieces of legislation were the Resource Conservation and

Recovery Act of 1976 (RCRA), which regulates the treatment, storage, disposal, and transportation of both hazardous and nonhazardous solid wastes, and the Comprehensive Emergency Response, Compensation and Liability Act of 1980 (CERCLA, also known as Superfund), which requires the cleanup of abandoned hazardous-waste sites. With the introduction of RCRA and CERCLA, and subsequent reauthorizations and amendments to all the major environmental laws, the commercial laboratory industry grew rapidly. Most observers of the environmental testing industry believe that the industry began to plateau starting in 1988 or 1989. Growth rates averaging 25 percent or more during the mid-1980s have slowed to around 5 percent currently.

The current size of the commercial market for environmental testing services is probably between $1.5 billion and $1.6 billion, with annual revenue growth being less than 5 percent. Testing under RCRA accounts for about half of total industry revenues, Superfund (CERCLA) another 20 percent, CWA 15 percent, and SDWA 5 percent, with the balance being divided among various other environmental statutes. Estimates of the current U.S. environmental instrument market are about $500 million.

The number of environmental testing laboratories in the United States is between 1,400 and 1,600, virtually all of these small. Of these, only 25 to 30 environmental testing labs generate revenues greater than $10 million. This is because market demand is generally local (markets are small) and economies of scope and scale, which could enable larger companies to compete at lower cost, are not evident. While there are many small testing laboratories because of low barriers to entry, the proven lack of economies of scale and scope limit their growth prospects.

In contrast, the equipment industry that serves the testing laboratories is markedly less fragmented and is a global opportunity. The top three environmental instrument manufacturers—Hewlett-Packard, Perkin-Elmer, and Thermo Instrument Systems—together account for almost 30 percent of environmental instrument sales globally. Small instrumentation manufacturers, of which there are probably several dozen in the United States, tend to specialize in niche markets (for example, waste water samplers) or emerging technologies (for example, field testing technologies).

Because the market for environmental testing services is created primarily by regulation and driven by enforcement, the entire population of laboratories is subject to a substantial degree of non-technological (and nonmarket) risk—specifically, the uncertainty inherent in the fits and starts of a political and regulatory process that effectively defines their market and determines their growth rate.

Equally, the inflexibility inherent in these regulatory schemes decreases the incentives for environmental testing labs and instrument suppliers to be innovative technologically. Indeed, environmental testing labs are unique in this respect, in that it is the only sector studied in this project where technological risk is almost entirely absent. In many cases regulations preclude proprietary "product" technologies; regulation of testing processes reduces technological uncertainty in the market for services and limits the potential benefits of small company innovation. As a consequence, current technical innovation in environmental testing labs focuses on incremental approaches to cost savings and throughput increases rather than new product development, which is largely irrelevant. In contrast to environmental testing labs, some forces do continue to drive innovation by instrument suppliers. There is an active R&D effort in new technologies and new applications of existing technologies to enable labs to reduce cost and improve flexibility through (1) improved information management systems, (2) increased automation, and (3) increased use of portable "field testing" technologies. As well, as the number of regulated compounds increases, the limitations of existing methods for various analyses may require the increased application of newer technologies, such as high-pressure liquid chromatography, liquid chromatography linked with mass spectroscopy, and sequential mass spectroscopy—although none of these technologies, for the most part, represents "cutting edge" science.

In summary, although environmental testing labs are technically oriented, demand for environmental testing services is created almost entirely by regulation and driven by enforcement; without these labs, aspects of current environmental regulation simply are not possible. This, in turn, introduces a high degree of risk for these labs, inherent in changes to this regulatory scheme. Consequently technological innovation tends to be incremental and to focus on cost savings. The overwhelming majority of environmental testing labs are also quite small. This reflects extremely low barriers to entry but also barriers to growth—no marked economies of scale have yet been demonstrated by environmental testing labs, and demand tends to be local. In contrast, the equipment industry that serves the testing labs is considerably less fragmented and is the locus of most R&D expenditures for the industry and the source of most process innovation.

Network Services and Access Devices

The consent decree that broke up the Bell system in 1982 had profound and far-reaching impacts in telecommunications by deregulating the long-distance telephone business. In parallel, that decade witnessed revolutionary improvements in computer technology, fiber-optic communications, and ability to communicate digital information at high rates on copper wires. These events in combination ushered in the "information age" in which we live. Over time, we have seen the merging of the wide area and local area networks and the expansion of other communications media with wireless ground and satellite-based technologies. As a result, enormous opportunities were opened for successful new businesses, and many companies have sprung up providing services or equipment or software (or a combination) in the general industry categories broadly denoted "telecommunications," "data communications," and "networking."

Among the earliest beneficiaries of deregulation were a host of new long-distance telephone service providers who, with modest capital, were able to underprice AT&T. After some years, these companies were acquired and consolidated into larger entities, such as LCI and LDDS, competing in the same markets with giants such as MCI (an early start-up), Sprint, and AT&T. Starting such a long-distance carrier is no longer a realistic business opportunity as costs favor the large players and pricing has become extremely competitive. On the device and system side, new companies grew up providing network access products and related software. Telco Systems, Inc., Newbridge Networks Corporation, Cisco, 3Com Corporation, Level 1 Communications, and SynOptics are examples of such successful companies, but there are many others. Note that these companies thrived despite the presence of established computer companies in the network equipment market, such as IBM and Digital Equipment Company, by providing new products tailored for emerging market segments.

Opportunities in these industries are being pursued by companies of all sizes that are capable of creating or combining software and physical assets to create networks and deliver services over those networks. This industry's fuzzy boundaries, its overlapping and competing technologies, its many participants, and its rapid growth rate make meaningful estimates of total size impossible, but it is very large. As indicators it is worth noting that annual U.S. local phone service revenues are about $80 billion, cable TV revenues exceed $20 billion, and "small" equipment markets—such as the market for video conferencing equipment—are conservatively projected to grow at 20 to 30 percent for the next several years.

The dramatic growth of networks both fuels and is fueled by dramatic fragmentation of opportunities. Much of the incremental development of networking technologies (as opposed to fundamental advances, such as optical transmission) required to realize new opportunities is done by new companies or entrepreneurs. In this industry small companies fill important niche markets and explore market acceptability for products considered too risky for larger companies:

• New companies are expected to play a key role in the viability of portable computing. The number of people using cellular and satellite systems to transmit data is anticipated to increase from less than million users in 1993 to more than 20 million users in the next decade. These broadband, interactive video and data services especially are seen as an opportunity for new companies, because the demand for these services is unrealized. This capability is also expected to create demand for new wireless devices such as keypads, integrated devices for voice and data, and future generations of personal digital assistants (PDAs) like Apple's Newton, which link cellular, wireless fax, and e-mail.

• Satellites are a spectacular demonstration of advance in information technology, creating the opportunity to provide instantaneous point-to-point communications or broadcast to anywhere on the globe. While satellite networks are mostly a large company proposition, the terminal devices for many satellite services, including positioning and navigation devices, and the personal digital devices needed to receive facsimile and data are expected to be developed by new companies at least initially. The terminal devices for the Global Positioning System, or GPS, for example, have been developed largely by small companies.

• The demand for broadband services, including full-motion video or multimedia, is creating demand for new, faster networking technologies. Existing local networks such as Ethernet, token ring, and fiber distributed data interface (FDDI) will eventually make the transition to faster technologies, such as asynchronous transfer mode (ATM) or "fast Ethernet." Implementation of these new broadband network technologies is creating enormous innovation in network equipment vendors, many of these by small or new companies.

Uncertainty about information network architectures and standards shapes the opportunity for start-ups in network devices. Because standards are in flux, it is still possible for a small company to set a *de facto* industry standard. Network devices and services are embedded in the telecommunications industry, an industry that has historically been heavily regulated—for example, in spectrum allocation, antitrust, and pricing. In this context, the absence (often temporary) of standards, including even proprietary standards, has encouraged innovation in network devices. This has created opportunities for small companies that are willing to accept a high level of risk, and simultaneously has discouraged larger competitors.

In summary, a high degree of commercial and technological uncertainty is forcing the larger players in networking to engage in a frenzied competitive search for solutions that simultaneously create *de facto* technical standards and establish the proprietary network technologies that will dominate the nation's information infrastructure. In this competitive environment, larger competitors depend on small companies to realize new opportunities that will drive demand for (a) communications capacity in these new networks, as well as (b) the core technologies such as compression technologies and portable computing.

Outdoor Sporting Goods

The $4 billion to $6 billion U.S. outdoor sporting goods industry—including backpacks, climbing ropes, kayaks, tents, and ski parkas, to name a few items—is nested within the larger industry of general sporting goods. These sporting goods markets are dominated by small privately-held companies—perhaps 5 percent are public companies, and only six of these have a market capitalization of over $1 billion. Many of the markets these companies serve grow rapidly with the growth of a particular sport; it is not unusual for sport participation to grow rapidly for several years. For example, in the early 1990s participation in two sports—rock climbing and in-line skating—grew at more than 20 percent a year for several years in a row.

The outdoor sporting goods industry—especially in "hot" sports—is characterized by innovation-oriented start-ups. The costs of entry are fairly low, opportunities for the application of new technology (often new materials technology) exist, and markets are fragmented and often small enough not to be of interest to larger companies. Further, the outdoor sporting goods industry is one in which user-inventors and trendsetters traditionally play a large role. In outdoor sporting goods, a climber, hiker, or paddler envisions a product he or she would like to have, creates a prototype in the basement, and manages to grow a company on the strength of a product that others, with similar experience to that of the inventor, appreciate. The result is that many companies in the industry have a strong predisposition to plan on product innovation as part of their company strategy. This is in marked contrast to process innovation, which tends to happen only in response to product and volume requirements.

Innovation in the outdoor sporting goods industry is typical of consumer product industries where the line between changing fashion and advancing product technology is usually blurred. Innovation in outdoor footwear is an excellent example. In the past decade hiking boots have become lighter while becoming more waterproof, easier to break-in, and easier to care for. Following the trend in athletic shoes, outdoor footwear has been revolutionized by new materials. Anyone who has ever broken in a old-style pair of heavy leather hiking boots will immediately recognize the technological advances inherent in the new, lighter generation of footwear. The dramatic increases in sales of the product, however, cannot be attributed simply to the technical superiority of the new boots. Lifestyle changes—an increase in the number of people walking on forest trails for recreation—are important. Even more important to the growth in sales are fashion changes; industry watchers are aware of the shift from "white" to "brown" shoes in the preferences of U.S. junior high students. Similarly, "amphibious" sandals—designed originally for rafting and other water sports—have evolved from clumsy special-purpose shoes into multipurpose outdoor footwear. While there is technical advance in the construction of the sandals, it is nonetheless an evolution driven by fashion. Similarly, while rollerskates are an old product, the rapidly growing sport of in-line skating ("blades" rather than "skates") was created out of innovation in materials and industrial design that allowed people to skate smoothly on concrete and asphalt. In short, innovation in many outdoor sporting goods is most important, and most prevalent, when it reinforces or responds to lifestyle and fashion changes.

Companies in the industry remain technically innovative—largely without much organized research, materials testing, product development, and product testing—by relying heavily on a small cadre of designers and innovators. A few "product designers" in these companies make virtually all decisions about aesthetics, structural characteristics, manufacturability, raw material specs and purchasing, pricing, testing, presentation, and shipping. The concentration of product and manufacturing process development in a few product designers also affects the organization of market research. Companies count on the personal outdoor experience of a few designers with the products to stay close to the market. Similarly, they count on the creativity of the same group to bring new technology (usually first developed outside the industry) to bear on either products or manufacturing processes.

In other words, the size of the companies, and of the markets most companies serve, pushes to keep the product development costs low and the various design functions centralized. At the same time the technical characteristics of the products are such that it is possible for a single individual, or a couple of individuals, to execute most or all of the design functions. The "personal" nature of most of the products, and the fact that many designers are outdoor enthusiasts, allows product development decision making to be centralized in people close to these markets. Additionally, executives in the industry refer to the necessity of maintaining advanced design and technology as well as a "feel" for the products and the industry.

Many of the small companies in the outdoor industry are best characterized as lifestyle companies. A single founder or small team of individuals creates a company (or buys an existing company) out of commitment to the sport and an interest in being a long-term participant in the industry. In sharp contrast to software start-ups, for example, many small companies in the industry— even the most innovation-oriented companies—do not expect to grow rapidly or to go public or be purchased by a larger company as a method of getting founders "liquid." Technical entrepreneurs in the industry are drawn primarily from the ranks of enthusiasts who want to be a part of the industry rather than from general entrepreneurs who see the industry as ripe for innovation-based businesses.

Finally, among the industries studied for this project, with the possible exception of prepackaged software, this industry is most dependent on established distribution and retail networks. Retail consolidation may increasingly squeeze small manufacturers as some retailers attain the volume necessary to integrate backward profitably into production; innovation may shift away from product design toward production cost savings.

In summary, the outdoor sporting goods industry is typical of a consumer product industry dominated by small companies. There is a considerable degree of technical entrepreneurship, the impacts of which are often indistinguishable from the impact of lifestyle and fashion trends. The industry is fragmented, with substantial pockets of technical dynamism and rapidly growing markets, but the expectations of entrepreneurs, and therefore the shape of the companies they build, are different from those in industries such as software or network devices.

Summary Comparison

The industries addressed in this study illustrate the diverse roles that small technically oriented companies play in an industry and in the economy.

Small companies in the software and the network devices and services industries are prototypical entrepreneurial high-tech companies. New technologies and new potential markets seem to create a wide range of opportunities in these industries for technically capable risk takers. Also, new company starts are supported by (a) relative ease of entry because of relatively low initial capital requirements; (b) a significant number of public business successes to encourage entrepreneurs to enter the industry; (c) companies that appear to have substantial value if sold, even though they are not necessarily long-term survivors; (d) availability of venture capital financing; and (e) a public market for the shares of companies at relatively high valuations, compared with other industries, on the basis of revenues or profitability. In both of these industries there are large, dominant companies, but the technological dynamism and fragmentation of the market create opportunities for small companies. **In both software and network industries the development and commercial proof of a wide range of emerging technologies, as well as the development and growth of the industry, depend on the investments and actions of small companies willing to take linked technological and business risks.**

Small companies play an unusual role in the advanced display industry. In the early 1990s technological uncertainty, widely expected but unrealized large markets, and government (Department of Defense) funding created a cadre of small relatively research-intensive companies in search of a valuable proprietary technological position. As evidenced by the high rate of partnerships with large companies, most small companies do not expect to be able to exploit such a proprietary position alone; the capital requirements of scale-up and manufacturing for large markets prevent most small companies from entering high-volume markets. **In the advanced display industry, small companies have been the repository of technical capability during the development of both core and complementary technologies and products. The cost of manufacturing facilities and the demands of process research and refinement suggest that these products will have to be produced by larger companies or partnerships.**

While there are considerable differences between outdoor sporting goods and implantable and surgical medical devices, some similarities stand out. In particular, user-inventors in both industries play an important role in bringing new products to market. In both industries small companies and user-inventors have provided innovation and product diversity in small markets. Moreover, in both industries most of the new technology that becomes part of a new commercial product comes from outside the industry itself. The considerable differences are also evident. In medical device innovation, most user-inventors are highly technically trained, the "field testing" of products is often a formal clinical trial in a university hospital, and, historically, venture capital was widely available for medical device start-ups. Further, medical devices are sold to physicians (and increasingly to health care organizations) rather than retailed directly to consumers and, of course, they are increasingly regulated by the FDA, a change that industry observers believe may alter forever the way medical device innovation is done and, perhaps, eliminate small company participation. **The outdoor sporting goods industry and the implantable and surgical medical device industry illustrate the range of small markets that are served by small innovation-oriented companies that often pull fundamental technical advance from outside the industry into new applications.**

Among the industries addressed by this study, environmental testing services stands alone. The industry is, indeed, a technically oriented industry dominated by small companies, but it has a unique characteristic because demand for services is created by regulation and driven by enforcement. Barriers to entry into the industry are low but so are the opportunities for growth; economies of scale, if they exist at all, are small and the opportunities for innovation are slight. However, environmental testing laboratories serve an important public function. Without good testing services, environmental regulation, and some aspects of environmental protection, would not be possible. In this sense, **environmental testing laboratories are small companies that serve the economy by providing an important technical service in small geographically differentiated markets.**

CONCLUSIONS

As the industries studied for this project show, small high-tech companies play a critical and diverse role in creating new products and services, in developing industries, and in driving technological change and growth in the U.S. economy. The contribution of these companies is not adequately measured by their R&D expenditures, their employment, or their contribution to the national storehouse of published or patented technical know-how. Pioneering new markets and providing innovation in small markets are often inherently risky activities and may yield economic returns that, for larger companies, are not commensurate with the risk.

In consumer markets, substantial benefits of linked commercial and technological risk taking—the rapid exploration of market potentials, the development and refinement of new products and services, certain types of technical innovation, and product diversity—accrue directly and immediately to individual consumers and to the national economy.

In intermediate or industrial markets, the willingness of small companies to shoulder technological and related market risks may enable other companies (both large and small) to pursue otherwise unavailable technological approaches to improving productivity or introducing new products. In small consumer and intermediate markets—slowly growing markets with total annual demand in the tens of millions rather than hundreds of millions of dollars—small companies are often the only source of products or services and, therefore, responsible for all product diversity and for bringing innovations to the market.

These market functions are an important part of industry and national economic development and, as such, are key in the economy's learning process about which technologies, at what price, will or will not satisfy demand.

As a consequence of different types and levels of business risk, however, small companies and start-ups fulfill market development functions in different ways in different sectors of the economy. Generalizing on the industries addressed in this study, the specific contributions of small technically oriented companies in an industry depend on the following factors:

• The size of markets, current and prospective, that make up the industry.

• The degree of technical uncertainty in current or prospective markets.

• The economies of scale and scope in production for a market.

• The dominance (or lack thereof) of larger companies in both final and intermediate markets in the industry.

It is important to emphasize the last point—that many high-tech opportunities for small companies depend intimately on the current structure and operations of large companies in an industry. For example, economies of scale and scope in the aircraft industry exclude start-up companies from the business of bringing a new airframe to market. It is, however, the structure and operation of large airframe manufacturers that determine whether a small high-tech company can supply new materials or advanced software to the industry.

Further, there is often a bias in large companies against certain types of technical investments; although large companies and small companies may see the same technological needs and opportunities, they perceive risk and make investment decisions differently. For example, large companies often do not address small markets on which they might make an acceptable level of return on investment, because the absolute value of the reward is insufficient to be noticeable on the company's books or because it cannot be quantified—the return on investment is not initially known for "seminal" investments, and so larger companies do not pursue them. Incremental investment decisions by large companies are likely to focus first on improvements in existing businesses and second on entering markets that have a good prospect of growth to a substantial size. From the perspective of a large company, this allows them to focus and to share with other companies some of the technological risk of improving their current business.

Based on the industries addressed in this study, the committee concludes that small technically oriented companies often assume types of risk (and an amount of risk) that is not usually tolerated by large companies. In the United States both consumers and companies often depend on small high-tech companies to explore the commercial application of technology in potential, emerging, and small markets. **The principal economic function of small entrepreneurial high-tech companies is to probe, explore, and sometimes develop the frontiers of the U.S. economy—products, services, technologies, markets—in search of unrecognized or otherwise ignored opportunities for economic growth and development.**

4

Opportunities for Small Technology-Oriented Companies

Technological entrepreneurial opportunities often depend on the ability of companies to tolerate high risk of financial failure, to be technologically creative and flexible. Further, the opportunities for small companies are intimately related to the activities of large companies and are heavily dependent on local or regional resources and business environment. Each of these determinants of the opportunity set for small technically oriented companies is discussed in this chapter.

HOW THE MARKET DETERMINES OPPORTUNITIES AND RISKS

Small companies exist in most industries, but they exist in abundance in industries that share the following characteristics:

- Fragmented, technically dynamic, and rapidly growing markets.
- Low barriers to entry.
- An adequate regional and national technical and business infrastructure.
- Good access to potential customers.
- Availability of financing.
- A culture (recent history) of entrepreneurship in the industry.

Where these conditions exist, they are often accompanied by a predicable set of business and technological risks. Business failure is common among start-ups, but it is the ability to identify and address opportunities while managing the characteristic risks that determines the success of new ventures.

Fragmented, Technically Dynamic, and Rapidly Growing Markets

Fragmentation of an industry into many markets, especially small and rapidly growing markets, generally means that there is limited competition from larger companies, few standards, and constantly changing opportunities for companies that can take a new approach.

The software industry and the network services and devices industries are excellent examples of fragmentation in technically dynamic and rapidly growing markets. While there is agreement that software and network services have tremendous potential, there continues to be a high degree of uncertainty about what applications consumers are willing to pay for and the features that will make or break those applications. Indeed, the high degree of uncertainty has seen almost all larger competitors adopt a "fast follower" strategy that avoids the high costs of developing a new market (and the potential cost of product failure). Instead, demand for the overwhelming majority of new software and network applications is likely to be discovered by innovative new companies and entrepreneurs.

Large companies and universities are often part of the business environment that creates and drives technically dynamic and fragmented industries. Larger companies are often inadvertently the source of start-ups in such industries in that they both create new niches and leave them unaddressed. Larger competitors also may have difficulties maintaining their intellectual capital as opportunities are perceived for entrepreneurs to go out on their own. Entrepreneurship in advanced displays and network devices, for example, is driven largely by spin-outs of corporate (and academic) talent.

In some industries, such as biotechnology, university-based research is a large portion of the total technical work in the area and therefore a prime contributor to the technical dynamism of the industry. However, even those sectors where there is little interaction between start-ups and universities often depend on academic research in engineering or basic sciences that have an indirect impact on industrial technology.

Universities are important as a source of ideas and talent in the most technically dynamic industries. For example, small software companies (as well as large companies) benefit from extensive networks of universities and research facilities, especially in Boston and the San Francisco Bay area. Small companies are the beneficiaries of the talent and intellectual capital that is concentrated in these areas, and they are often the incubators for further development and application of advanced concepts developed at universities, usually through graduates and faculty who join the firm.

In sum, technically dynamic, fragmented, and rapidly growing markets attract technical entrepreneurs. Large companies and universities help fuel those markets with technological ideas and talent.

Low Barriers To Entry

Traditional barriers to entry, such as high up-front capital costs or a proprietary technology held by a competitor, are critical problems for small high-tech companies. Industries and industry segments in which barriers to entry are low attract entrepreneurs. For technically oriented start-ups low barriers to entry can simply mean that one or two technical professionals can lead a team to make a potentially useful incremental technical contribution. In outdoor sporting goods, for example, most products are "personal" or small-scale one-user products. The characteristics of these products—in contrast to an automobile, an airplane, or a microprocessor—are that product and process design and development can be handled by a small team. A single, talented individual can execute the market and technical research, product development and design, prototyping, field testing, and redesign of products in a way that is not possible for larger, more complex products.

Low barriers to entry are often associated with a marked absence of economies of scale in some high-value-added aspect of the business. In environmental testing, for example, the economics appear to oppose consolidation. Virtually all companies in the environmental testing sector are small. This is because market demand is generally local and economies of scale in environmental laboratory services appear to be minimal. In these instances, specialization in a focused geographic area may realize substantial economies, but the absence of larger economies of scale (or perhaps even diseconomies) precludes larger competitors from consolidating the industry.

A type of diseconomy of scale arises from the difficulty of large organizations in exploiting fragmented markets. Small companies enjoy a comparative advantage in opportunities that demand rapid product changes or style changes, as in outdoor sporting goods or medical devices. Outdoor sporting goods and implantable and surgical medical devices are similar in that the inventors and company founders are often themselves intense users of the innovations. Product development is also similar in that it is usually iterative and experimental, it directly involves the user, and there is often little benefit to larger size or organization for product development.

An Adequate Technical and Business Infrastructure

Small companies and start-ups rarely "go it alone." In general, small companies need to draw on technical and business resources outside the company. With regard to business matters, technical small companies and start-ups often depend—for advice and direct help—on an infrastructure of business services such as legal, accounting, and banking services. With regard to technical matters, small companies rarely do any self-supported research (though the biotechnology industry is an exception in this regard). Small technical companies almost always depend on technical advances made in large company laboratories or in universities and the importance of that infrastructure is most clearly revealed when it is unavailable.[1] Further, much of the technical talent that small companies draw on is trained in larger companies or universities.

---

[1] For example, access to materials technologies used in medical devices and sporting goods is increasingly restricted in response to fears of liability litigation. A case in point is DuPont's Dacron polyester. The total market for this product is approximately $9 billion per year, but the cost of polyester used in a popular medical device is often only several hundred thousand dollars per year. As a result, the major suppliers of polymers used for medical devices have severely restricted the use of these materials.

Innovation in implantable and surgical medical devices is an interesting example of this. Most of the enabling technical advances that make small-company product innovation possible (new materials or electronic controls, for example) migrate into medical devices from other industries or applications. The products are often conceived, developed, and tested by a sophisticated cadre of clinical professionals (physicians, often university-based) who are constantly developing insights into better ways to do things as a function of their daily clinical experience. The business and technical infrastructure for most small implantable and surgical medical devices is clustered primarily around the nation's teaching hospitals and is supported by substantial federal research funds.

Good Access To Potential Customers

A technologically oriented small company or start-up needs early customers as a way of learning about actual use of a product or service as part of the product development process. Beyond early customer trials, customer access, and the cost of that access, is a key determinant of success and growth rate. Even clearly superior products will rarely succeed unless they can get "shelf space." The market for home network services, for example, is highly fragmented and unsettled, but access to the customer depends on a few large companies, primarily cable companies and telephone companies. Small technically oriented companies, therefore, depend on arrangements with these large companies to test the viability of services and products. For small companies, good access to customers often has a great deal to do with their relationships with large companies—either directly as customers or as vehicles for reaching the ultimate customer.

In the medical device industry, there is a revolution in customer access that is challenging the industry's ingenuity. Historically there was a decentralized system for testing and adoption—individual physicians made most of the decisions. With the increasing consolidation of health care providers and the movement toward health care reform, the customer is increasingly a health care company or insurance provider. The methods of customer access for device innovators—either for product development and refinement or for post-refinement sales—is changing in a way that may disadvantage small, thinly capitalized companies.

Availability of Financing

Small companies depend on both debt and equity financing. Debt financing, and its availability from banks or finance companies, is an issue of almost chronic concern for both small business advocates and government policymakers. Small Business Administration loan programs, certain bank regulatory changes, and proposals for a federal role in creating a secondary market for business loans are all driven by concerns about small business access to debt financing. Because of the nature of much technological development, however, small technologically oriented companies depend heavily on equity financing for development of new products and services and for market development.

Many technology-dependent ventures are poor candidates for debt financing. The investments are illiquid, slow to mature, and hard to manage. The risk/return profile of such investments more closely matches the interests of a certain category of equity investors. In most cases equity financing is provided by savings or by family and friends, but in some cases outside venture investors play a key role. For both the entrepreneur (operator-investor) and the outside investor, the willingness to invest depends on a variety of factors, not the least of which are the four industry conditions described above. In addition to the initial conditions of the opportunity, equity investors are deeply interested in potential return at exit. In industries rich in opportunities for small companies and start-ups, the interest of entrepreneurial talent and outside investors depends on the likelihood of getting a good "liquid" return in a time frame determined by the investor's interests.

Although owner-operators and their close associates provide equity in virtually all industries, the availability of equity financing from professional venture capital investors is directly related to expected growth rate of a venture, the expected potential market, and the perceived ability of a company to capture share in this market. These factors—and recent experiences in the industry—determine the anticipated liquidity of equity investment. In this context, liquidity is relative: Can an investor's interest in a company be sold relatively quickly and at a good price?

The large number of start-ups and small companies in network devices and in software is an example of this. Organized venture capital is currently often available to companies in these sectors, because quickly increasing or nascent opportunities create liquidity; initial public offerings of the stock of companies in these industries are often well received because of expectations of rapid growth. These opportunities that small companies exploit are also attractive to larger competitors once the opportunity is demonstrated, creating liquidity through acquisition and encouraging the formation of new companies.

In environmental testing laboratories and outdoor sporting goods, on the other hand, the story is quite different. In environmental testing labs, for example, poor liquidity creates barriers to exit for entrepreneurs. Because the economics of environmental testing appear to discourage consolidation (by acquisition or expansion), there is effectively no market clearing function, so some competitors will stay in the industry simply because they cannot exit at what they consider to be a fair price. Such limited near-term opportunity precludes venture capital financing. As a consequence, equity financing for start-ups or expansion in environmental testing labs is most likely to come primarily from owner-operators, not from external sources. Similarly in sporting goods, branding can create liquidity for even small companies, but sporting goods markets are often small and with limited growth possibilities.

Indeed, even if the liquidity is good, the potential market needed to justify an investment increases as the requirements for resources and capital increase. For example, venture capital financing of implantable and surgical medical devices, historically quite active, has deteriorated dramatically as the time (and cost) for moving from start-up to successful company has increased substantially because of changes in device approval processes. In many cases, this shifts the burden of financing innovative investments to larger companies that may be able to reduce the risk (through their experience with the regulatory system) and can justify a slower or lower device-specific return because the investment is part of an overall plan for corporate growth and development.

In advanced displays, liquidity is also a concern. The number of small technology-intensive companies in advanced displays reflects technological issues and the fact that companies do not have access to the capital required to grow through large-scale production.

A Culture (Recent History) of Entrepreneurship

Industries are also differentiated by the degree of social acceptance of entrepreneurship. In some cases the social acceptance of entrepreneurship is created by example: entrepreneurial dreams are most prevalent in industries in which there are visible successes, in which a few individuals have built big companies from scratch or become fabulously wealthy. In other cases, the acceptability of entrepreneurship is more ambiguous. Medical device innovation, for example, reflects a relatively new currency of academic values in the life sciences, where the profit motive was previously seen as antithetical to academia. In recent years it has become much more acceptable for academically oriented life science professionals to be involved in start-ups.

Entrepreneurship may also be a lifestyle decision based on doing what you enjoy, and being your own boss, as in outdoor sporting goods, where many companies are founded by enthusiasts. Entrepreneurship in software is often similarly a lifestyle decision, usually in the negative sense ("I could *never* work for a big company"), and fueled by the fact that many people in the industry believe it is fairly easy to start a company that may not become large but can quickly create significant equity value because of its technical sophistication. Software and services attracted more venture capital financing than any other sector, 22 percent of venture capital invested in 1992, or $562 million in 214 different companies.[2]

Characteristic Risks

Technological and market acceptance risks—the usual risks of any commercial technological development—are important in technically dynamic markets. Will a particular application of new technology gain adequate market acceptance? How long will it take to develop market demand for a product or service with unusual characteristics or function? The typical risk is heightened in fragmented, technically dynamic, and rapidly growing markets by the

---

[2]Venture Economics, *The National Venture Capital Association 1993 Annual Report* (Washington, D.C.: National Venture Capital Association, 1994).

fact there are often few firm standards and little customer experience with the product or service. It is easy to develop a product or service that becomes rapidly obsolete in these markets because of changing standards. Similarly, without good customer feedback on product development paths, it is easy to bring out products or services for which there is little demand.

Although low barriers to entry provide opportunity for start-ups, they also make it difficult for small companies to establish much durable competitive advantage—either against other new entrants or against larger companies. Industries in which perceived barriers to entry are low (the software industry, for example), are often characterized by fierce competition; perhaps the dominant risk for small companies in low-barrier-to-entry markets is the risk of chronic exposure to high levels of direct competition.

The industries addressed in this study illustrate how the characteristics of a product or service market are key determinants of small business technological opportunity; the demands of successful commercial innovation in different markets differ, leading to varied levels of expenditures on research, development, demonstration, and to variation in the organization of company technical effort. Small companies have inherent advantages in fragmented, technically dynamic, and rapidly growing markets in which there are low barriers to entry. The rapid pace of change in such business environments often creates nascent or rapidly growing markets where a small company may establish an early position by luck or skill simply because the opportunity is new.

THE LARGE-COMPANY ROLE

The interactions between new, technology-intensive companies and larger companies are myriad, diverse, and critical to the growth of many industries. There is an excellent analogy to the biological concept of coevolution; populations do not exist in isolation, but interact with other populations, and these interactions shape the opportunities for each population. Small companies, equally, do not exist in isolation but interact with larger companies.

Extending the biological analogy, it is easy to see a variety of economic or organizational rationales for the interdependence of large- and small-company technological opportunities. First, in some technological areas, there are no large companies that can reasonably exploit a radical new technology, often still in the process of emerging from basic science. The biotechnology industry, for example, has been driven mainly by advances in university research environments. In the early days of the industry, large pharmaceutical companies did not have the competence in biotechnology to drive research and development. Start-ups bridged the gap and, simultaneously, captured a large portion of the available talent.

In other industries, the breadth, depth and uncertainty of technological advance drive large companies to accept that much of the development and market testing will be done by small companies and technological start-ups. For example, even large telecommunications companies see too many potential growth markets and too much uncertainty to exploit the full range of network product and service markets. The expectation that agile, small companies will explore markets, some of which will become large, is probably the source of the large numbers of joint ventures between large and small companies in this industry. Large companies also quite inadvertently leave gaps and ignore technological opportunities. For example, the dominant computer companies in the early 1980s failed to see the opportunity in personal computers and left the pioneering of that market to a number of start-ups, including Apple Computer.

Second, in many cases technological and market opportunities are simply not attractive to large companies. The opportunities in several sectors examined in this study—medical devices, sporting goods, environmental testing labs—are not necessarily attractive to larger companies. Barriers to entry for start-ups and small companies are relatively low and opportunities tend to be small or highly fragmented. In these circumstances, a small company's comparative advantage is the willingness of owners to be happy serving a small market.

Lack of economies of scale—or the existence of diseconomies of scale—can preclude entry by larger companies. In environmental testing, for example, the economics appear to discourage consolidation. Although the total opportunity is large, virtually all companies in the environmental testing sector are small. This is because market demand is generally local and economies of scale in laboratory services appear to be minimal. In these instances, specialization in a focused geographic area may realize substantial economies, but the absence of larger economies of scale precludes larger competitors from consolidating the industry.

High product differentiation, especially if based on image, also creates opportunities for small companies. If product differentiation is high and based on image, as in sporting goods, it can effectively limit the size of the firm (larger size may not be compatible with the image or exclusivity of the product) and create an opportunity for inefficient smaller competitors to survive.

Based on the industries considered in this study, it is clear that, with regard to certain opportunities, small companies appear to enjoy several advantages over larger companies. For example, small companies may enjoy a comparative advantage in technological development opportunities that demand rapid and fairly fundamental changes in direction. Indeed, the size of the most able organization may be simultaneously determined with the characteristic of the opportunity. Companies in rapidly growing, fragmented, technically dynamic markets must be able to change direction quickly. Organizationally, it is simply easier to change direction in an organization with fewer controls or traditions of practice.

Additionally, small high-tech companies also appear to be better than larger companies at developing initial business opportunities in new technologies or applications that demand high creative content, such as software development or the design of a new medical device or sporting goods. It is hard for large companies to nurture creativity and innovation, and the ratio of reward to risk in new product development is typically low. Individual or small team creativity seems easier to manage in small companies, perhaps because it is easier to invest the creative individual or team directly with the rewards of accomplishment, whether those rewards are money or recognition. This is by no means universally true, as some large companies have a reputation for the small-scale innovativeness and rapid market testing that is more typical of high-tech start-ups.

Also, many large companies cannot or do not pursue technologies discovered or developed in-house. In many cases the technology does not fit naturally with their current product line, or the ultimate market does not appear large enough to warrant further investment. As a result, many successful new companies spin out of these larger technology-driven companies—entrepreneurship in advanced displays and network devices, for example, is driven largely by spin-outs of corporate (and academic) talent. This, in turn, is forcing adaptations in larger companies. In some instances the spin-out is encouraged and financed by the larger company.

Three points emerge from these considerations of small company and large company interactions. **First, it does not make sense to consider the comparative advantage of small companies without embedding that discussion in the context of a specific market sector or technology.** Small companies can exploit certain opportunities, but that set of opportunities is often at least partially determined by the actions of larger companies.

Second, the opportunities for small companies in a sector or technology are not static; the importance of entrepreneurial innovation in developing new technologies depends on timing. Typically, as an industry and its technology mature, the uncertainty decreases (as does risk), enabling larger companies to assess the attractiveness of the opportunity. As a result, larger firms become increasingly involved with small companies in driving innovation beyond a certain point.

Third, it is important to remember that small companies—except in unusual circumstances—do little research.[3] The importance of spin-outs of technology, personnel, and business opportunities from large company expenditures and efforts at research and development should not be underestimated as a source of opportunity for small companies.

THE IMPORTANCE OF GEOGRAPHY

Much high-tech, small company activity is regionally reinforcing. The ability of some regional economies to spawn new businesses is well recognized. The economic contributions of "Silicon Valley" in northern California and "Route 128" around Boston are legendary. The success of those two regions has spawned a host of

---

[3]Small biotechnology firms are exceptional in that a significant number do a great deal of true research. The industry employs a disproportionate number of scientists, and in the aggregate (i.e., including the several larger firms) expends upward of $5 billion annually for R&D. The exploratory nature of this research underlies the high failure rate of experimental biotech drugs in clinical trials.

studies aimed at uncovering the key contributing factors. More important, it has stimulated many regions to experiment with different methods of regional economic development in the hope of emulating the success in California and Massachusetts.

The literature on what causes a region to become a center of high-tech entrepreneurship is both broad and deep,[4] and there is general agreement about the basic contributing factors:

Regional Sources of Entrepreneurs and Ideas

• Technology-intensive universities, federal research laboratories, and nonprofit research institutes.
• Technology-intensive activities of existing larger corporations.

Factors Affecting the Start-ups in a Region

• Availability of cheap and functional space.
• Quality of relationships between start-ups and technology-intensive institutions.

---

[4]The literature on regional development and technology addresses two major questions: (1) what makes a region a particularly successful locus for high-tech start-ups? and (b) what technology-oriented regional development activities are effective at "modernization," or the diffusion of new technology and good practices to existing firms? The question about high-tech start-ups has been recently addressed in a book by AnneLee Saxenian, *Regional Advantage: Culture and Competition in Silicon Valley and Route 128* (Harvard University Press, 1994) and from different perspectives by Edward Roberts, *Entrepreneurs in High Technology: Lessons from MIT and Beyond* (Oxford University Press, 1991) and William Bygrave and Jeffery A. Timmons, *Venture Capital at the Crossroads* (Harvard Business School Press, 1992). The question about modernization is comprehensively addressed (for rural areas, at least) by Stuart Rosenfeld, *Competitive Manufacturing: New Strategies for Regional Development* (Center for Urban Policy Research/Rutgers University, 1992). While the two issues are often treated separately, the two economic activities are obviously closely related. This is illustrated by the policy-oriented publications that blend approaches to both activities, for example, Christopher Coburn, editor, *Partnerships: A Compendium of State and Federal Cooperative Technology Programs* (Battelle Memorial Institute, 1995) and Carnegie Commission on Science, Technology, and Government, *Science, Technology and the States in America's Third Century* (Carnegie Commission, 1992).

- Quality, availability, and entrepreneurial orientation of the technical workforce.
- Quality and experience of support professionals (lawyers, accountants, world-class technical and business consultants).
- Availability of a venture capital network that acts to winnow start-ups, fund companies, and reduce the risk of innovation by providing information and guidance to funded companies.
- The entrepreneurial culture and resources created by a sufficient density of technology-based start-ups in a region.
- Quality of life available to entrepreneurs, including resources for families, such as good primary and secondary schools.

Factors Affecting the Ability of a Company to Grow in a Region

- Transportation infrastructure.
- Availability of long-term equity investors and willingness and experience of banks to lend to growing technology-based companies.
- Quality, availability, and entrepreneurial orientation of the technical management workforce.
- Labor costs, energy costs, unionization, and a host of traditional "industrial location" criteria such as the cost of housing.

Furthermore, there is increasing awareness of both the predictable and unpredictable dynamic characteristics of regional, high-tech economic growth. Predictably, many of the resources that a region needs develop simultaneously, and success breeds success. For example:

- Much regional investment capital for an industry comes from individuals who live in the region and succeeded in a related industry—a few successful high-tech companies will help create local sources of finance.
- The willingness of individuals (including university faculty and students) to take the risks of starting a new company in the region will be profoundly affected by the visible successes (or lack thereof) of similar ventures over the course of the last couple of decades.
- The local support professionals (especially lawyers and accountants) will have the necessary expertise in high-tech start-ups

only if there are enough high-tech start-ups to justify the development of such expertise.

• As a company grows out of an inventor's garage, the ability to attract management talent to the still risky venture depends somewhat on the local economy for such talent. That is, if the venture fails, is there another job of comparable quality likely to be available?

The system is also unpredictable or, perhaps, accident prone. Because of the predictable synergies, a small, unpredictable event—the decision of a single founder to move a new business out of a region for personal reasons, for example—can have a profound impact on the long-term development of the region. What if William Hewlett and David Packard had decided 40 years ago to move their fledgling company to Ann Arbor, Michigan, or Portland, Oregon, in search of lower labor rates? What would Silicon Valley look like today without the business "children" of the Hewlett-Packard Company and the technical and management infrastructure that is continually re-created by the ongoing presence of this and other such companies? What if William Shockley had been a better businessman and founded a stable company and not one that, through its dissolution, created a pattern of spin-outs and start-ups that created the semiconductor industry in the United States? For all its sunshine and the presence of Stanford University, the Santa Clara Valley still depended on some happy accidents for its success and entrepreneurial character.

In summary, the vigor of entrepreneurial activity is determined in large measure by local and regional characteristics: sources of people and ideas, such as research universities and large corporate labs; supportive infrastructure, such as incubators, seed capital, entrepreneurial networks, and advisory services; and resources for company formation and growth, such as a strong technical and managerial workforce.

SUMMARY AND CONCLUSIONS

The premise of this chapter is that certain technological business opportunities can best be exploited by small technically oriented companies. The changing topography of a complex economy, such as the U.S. economy, will include market opportunities that draw technical entrepreneurs. In particular, technical entrepreneurship thrives in fragmented, technically dynamic, and rapidly growing markets with low barriers to entry. Additionally, though the catch phrase of the 1990s may well be "global" economy, it is often local or regional characteristics and resources that determine the number and success of small high-tech ventures.

Some opportunities for small companies are the product of single events—an unusual technical breakthrough or a policy change that dramatically alters the business landscape. More often such opportunities emerge from a set of interrelated factors that determine or circumscribe the opportunity set for small technically oriented companies irrespective of their internal motivations or capabilities. These factors include primarily (a) market and technological characteristics that determine the shape of individual venture opportunities and the nature of business and technological risk, and (b) the existence and action of larger companies as suppliers, buyers, and competitors.

5
How Governments Can Nurture Small Companies and Technological Innovators

Numerous federal, state, and local policy mechanisms, including federal R&D funding, technical assistance programs, business incubators, loan guarantee programs, and university-industry collaborative ventures promote small company formation and growth. These initiatives are motivated by a variety of objectives, including the desire to assist specific segments of the economy such as small businesses or high-tech companies.

As discussed earlier, this study did not specifically evaluate government programs to support small high-tech businesses. Rather, the committee has asked, How well do government policies (a) help technological innovation in small companies, or (b) inadvertently affect small high-tech companies (e.g., regulation or tax policy)? This section provides an overview of three types of federal policy mechanisms:[1]

---

[1]The material in this section is derived from several sources, including the *Economic Report of the President 1994* (U.S. Government Printing Office); *Guide to NIST* (U.S. Department of Commerce, Technology Administration, October 1993); *The State of Small Business: A Report of the President 1993* (U.S. Government Printing Office); *Small Business Innovation Development Act Tenth Annual Report 1993* (U.S. Small Business Administration Office of Innovation, Research, and Technology); and conversations with staff at the National Institute of Standards and Technology, the Small Business Administration, the Advanced Research Projects Agency, and the House Committee on Small Business.

- Those aimed at helping small business.
- Those aimed at fostering technology development.
- Those that assist companies that are both small and technology-intensive.

This chapter also provides an overview and examples of state and regional efforts.[2] The closing sections describe some of the unintentional effects of government policy on entrepreneurial, high-tech companies and proposes some basic principles for policies intended to encourage small high-tech company formation and operation in the United States.

Many of the policy mechanisms described in this chapter—either directly or indirectly—play an enormous role in creating and destroying opportunities in many sectors of the economy that depend for their development on small high-tech companies. Government programs that directly support R&D in advanced displays can reduce technological risk, for example. But the indirect consequences of government actions are often poorly understood by policymakers—compliance with health and safety regulations, for example, in many instances is especially difficult for small companies and start-ups. These indirect consequences of government policies on innovation, and the extreme diversity of external conditions for small technology-intensive companies, need to be carefully considered.

FEDERAL POLICIES: SMALL BUSINESS ASSISTANCE

The **Small Business Administration (SBA)** is the federal government's economic development agency for small business. The SBA's primary task is to guarantee loans, but it also provides procurement assistance and other business development programs and conducts research into the operations of small business. The SBA's second-largest program after loan guarantees is the **Small Business Development Centers (SBDC)** program. The program issues matching grants to participating academic, private, and pub-

---

[2]An excellent reference work on state technology activities is *Partnerships: A Compendium of State and Federal Cooperative Technology Programs*. Published by the Battelle Memorial Institute in 1995, the *Compendium* profiles the cooperative technology programs of the 50 states and 10 federal agencies.

lic institutions, of which there are more than 750 across the country, to provide training and counseling to sharpen management skills for owners of small businesses. The program also offers specialized services designed to meet local needs in the areas of international trade, procurement, rural development, and technical assistance. The SBA currently also has a cooperative agreement with the National Institute of Standards and Technology (NIST) to help the SBDCs access on-line technical and business information.

The SBA licenses **Small Business Investment Companies (SBICs)** to provide government-guaranteed loans and other types of financing to small companies that cannot obtain financing elsewhere. SBICs have invested more than $10 billion in nearly 70,000 small businesses. During the savings and loan crisis of the late 1980s, more than 160 of the SBICs were liquidated, in many cases because their assets were less than they had led the SBA to believe.

The **Small Business Innovation Research (SBIR)** program, which will be discussed below, provides competitive opportunities for small companies to win federal R&D contracts.

NIST administers the **Manufacturing Extension Partnership (MEP)** program, which promotes the commercialization of technologies and the diffusion of technological information. This program consists of four major elements: Manufacturing Technology Centers (MTCs), Manufacturing Outreach Centers (MOCs), the State Technology Extension Program (STEP), and LINKS.

The **Manufacturing Technology Centers** program was established in 1988 to help small- and medium-sized manufacturers upgrade their technological practices and performance. MTCs, of which there are currently seven across the country, are selected from competing proposals submitted by prospective sponsoring organizations. They provide a variety of services, including individual project engineering, training courses, demonstrations, and assistance in selecting and using software and equipment.

Awards for **Manufacturing Outreach Centers** started in FY1994. These centers, like the MTCs, help manufacturers adopt appropriate, modern technologies, but they offer more limited services. They will be affiliated with existing technical or training institutions, such as vocational institutes, technical colleges, state or university technical assistance centers, in areas not served by MTCs and with lower concentrations of industry. The **State Technology Extension Program** provides support to state and local technology-outreach organizations to enhance coordination among existing technology-assistance programs and help to improve delivery of those services. STEP grants, which are generally in the range of $50,000 to $200,000, are awarded to nonprofit institutions or organizations that must provide matching funds for the project.

The purpose of **LINKS** is to identify and "network" sources of assistance, information, and technology. A key feature is the electronic linkage of MTCs, MOCs, and other organizations such as federal laboratories and universities. Rapid communication and access to databases and information on manufacturing practices and technical experts in intended to be enabled by LINKS.

In addition, small businesses are the beneficiaries of contract set-asides from the federal government that totaled $12.9 billion in 1994 alone. The aim of such set-asides is to ensure that small businesses get a fair share of federal business. Among federal "quota" programs, the one for small businesses is by far the largest—the $12.9 billion in federal contract set-asides for small business in 1994 was double that for minority-owned businesses.

FEDERAL POLICIES: TECHNOLOGY INITIATIVES

Technology initiatives strive to promote the development and diffusion of growth- and productivity-enhancing technologies as well as correct market failures that would otherwise generate too little investment in R&D. In general these programs work by attempting (a) to share risks during start-up phases by providing partial funding for a technology development or refinement that is selected and also supported by the private sector; and (b) to stimulate the diffusion of new technologies among small firms by providing small amounts of resources and information. There are a number of programs in place to accomplish these purposes.

The **Advanced Technology Program (ATP)**, which is administered by the NIST, provides grants to industry consortia and start-up firms involved in precommercial R&D. The program helps firms develop breakthrough technologies that will have substantial long-term economic benefit but may be considered too risky by venture capitalists.

Projects are selected based on technical and business merit by independent panels of experts. The competition is rigorous. Single-company awards are limited to $2 million to be spent over no more than three years and must be used only for direct R&D costs. Joint ventures may receive up to $5 million, but they must also provide matching funds. The ATP supports development of laboratory prototypes and proof of technical feasibility but not commercial prototypes or proof of commercial feasibility. Award recipients are allowed to patent inventions or copyright software that is developed using ATP awards, but the government retains a nonexclusive license.

Begun in the 1990s, ATP has made 89 awards to 66 companies and 23 joint ventures since its inception. Including the private-sector funds, the awards have totaled $500 million. In 1994 it was announced that $745 million over the next five years would be dedicated to 11 strategic areas of technology: tools for DNA diagnostics, catalysis and biocatalysis technologies, materials processing for heavy manufacturing, motor vehicle manufacturing, advanced vapor-compression refrigeration, component-based software, digital video information networks, digital data storage, information infrastructure for health care, manufacturing composite structures, and computer-integrated manufacturing for electronics. Government investment in these strategic areas is expected to leverage an equal investment by industry. This support is in addition to ATP's general competition for all areas of technology. In 1995 Congress rescinded about $90 million in FY1995 funds from the ATP budget. As a result, NIST delayed the announcement and implementation of new focused programs and decreased the number FY1995 awardees.

Launched on March 11, 1993, the **Technology Reinvestment Project's (TRP)** mission is to promote the development of dual-use (commercial and military) technologies and to help small defense firms make the transition to commercial production. A six-agency council representing the Departments of Commerce, Energy, Transportation, and Defense, NASA, and the National Science Foundation implements the program. The TRP funds three types of projects: technology development, technology deployment to small businesses, and manufacturing education and training. As of December 1993, 162 projects had been selected for TRP support, totaling $1 billion in public and private funds.

The intent of **Cooperative Research and Development Agreements (CRADAs)** is to leverage the technical expertise resident in the country's 726 federal laboratories to enhance U.S. competitiveness through jointly financed collaborations with companies and industry consortia. The agreements cover joint research efforts in which both the federal lab and the cooperating company provide staff, equipment, facilities, or funds in any number of possible combinations. In the Department of Energy's 31 laboratories alone, there are 650 agreements totaling $1.4 billion in combined public and private funds.

The **Advanced Research Projects Agency (ARPA)** manages selected basic and applied research and development projects for the Department of Defense and pursues R&D in areas where there is high risk and payoff as well as significant potential for both military and commercial applications. ARPA does not carry out research in its own facilities but acts as a technology broker and venture capitalist by contracting work to industry, academia, and branches of the armed services. The FY1995 budget for ARPA was $2.6 billion.

FEDERAL PROGRAMS THAT SUPPORT
SMALL HIGH-TECH COMPANIES

The **Small Business Innovation Research** program, administered by the Small Business Administration, was established in 1982 and requires each federal agency with an external R&D budget of at least $100 million to set aside 2 percent of these research funds for SBIR in fiscal years 1995 and 1996 and 2.5 percent thereafter. Currently 11 federal agencies participate. According to the Tenth Annual Report on the Small Business Innovation Development Act, since the program's inception, 25,000 awards have been made to small high-tech companies worth more than $3.2 billion.

Each agency participating in the SBIR program issues a solicitation at least once a year indicating its R&D needs and inviting R&D proposals from small companies. In Phase I, small companies may apply for agency funding up to $100,000 for feasibility testing of an innovative idea or technology. In Phase II, award winners whose ideas show promise may receive up to $750,000 and two years to develop the concept. Following completion of Phase II, small companies are expected to obtain Phase III funding from private sources or non-SBIR federal sources to develop the concept into a commercial product. The SBA classifies SBIR awards into various technology areas. Roughly 36 percent of all SBIR awards made during the 1983-1992 period involved electronics, while another 36 percent were computer related.

A secondary but distinct program created by the 1992 Small Business Research and Development Enhancement Act is the **Research and Research & Development (R&R&D) Goaling Program**. Federal agencies with a fiscal year budget for research or research and development in excess of $20 million are required to establish small business goals for awarding R&R&D funding agreements to small companies. Seven other agencies, in addition to the 11 SBIR agencies, participate in the goaling program.

As part of the Small Business Research and Development Enhancement Act of 1992, the **Small Business Technology Transfer Program (STTR)** was established. This is a three-year pilot program at five federal agencies—Department of Defense, Department of Energy, Department of Health and Human Services, National Aeronautics and Space Administration, and the National Science Foundation—with extramural R&D budgets over $1 billion. The program was started in FY1994, with steadily increasing set-asides: 0.05 percent in FY1994, 0.10 percent in FY1995, and 0.15 percent in FY1996. It will peak in 1996 at $75 million. Under this plan, the federal government allocates the above percentages of its external R&D budget to fund cooperative R&D projects involving a small company and a researcher at a university, federal laboratory, or nonprofit research institution. Not less than 40 percent of the work must be performed by the small business and not less than 30 percent by the research institution; however, the small company is the primary contractor with overall management and performance responsibilities. The intent is to combine the entrepreneurial talent of small business and the innovative ideas of engineers and scientists in research institutions.

Like the SBIR, the STTR is a competitive, three-phased program. Phase I awards of $100,000 are to determine the scientific and technical merit and feasibility of an idea. The most promising Phase I efforts will be able to continue the research through a Phase II award, averaging $500,000. In Phase III, the awardees are expected to use private capital or non-SBTT funds to pursue commercial applications of the R&D.

The **Advanced Technology Program** is not explicitly targeted to smaller companies, but such companies are often the beneficiaries of the program. In the first three competitions, over half the

ATP awards were led by small companies with many more acting as subcontractors to larger company awardees.

A substantial number of participants in **CRADAs** are small firms, although this program as well is not specifically targeted to small companies. For example, approximately 44 percent of NIST's 250 CRADAs are with small businesses.

ARPA is a source of support for small business through its participation in the SBIR and TRP programs and through the granting of other R&D contracts.

STATE AND REGIONAL ASSISTANCE PROGRAMS

From a national perspective, the value of state and local economic development efforts are uneven. On the one hand, competition among states for plant location using tax breaks and economic development bonds may do little for the national economy. On the other hand, state and local manufacturing extension—the provision of management and technical assistance to small and medium-sized manufacturers—can be of considerable value, depending on how the programs are designed and managed. Also, state and local efforts to develop regional, technology-intensive, entrepreneurial economies do have the potential to strengthen the national economy and, perhaps, help drive technical innovation of value to consumers and citizens.

Each region's approach needs to be different and will depend on the region's current assets and weaknesses. A region with a high density of technical facilities of larger companies will need to develop different assets than one that has few such facilities but one or more first-rank technical universities. A region that has a strong tradition of skilled manufacturing (and therefore a regional density of skilled technical manufacturing personnel) will need to develop different assets than a region with little manufacturing history but with a substantial biological research institute.

State technology assistance programs, also referred to as technology or industrial extension programs, encompass a variety of initiatives offering assistance to small firms. Although not explicitly mandated to serve small companies, most of the firms using these services are small- or medium-sized companies. The funding is mixed, with state governments, universities, industry, and user fees providing most of the funding and federal government contributions making up the balance. The types of services provided include review of current or proposed manufacturing methods and processes, productivity and quality assessments, assistance with plant layout and operations, advice on the acquisition and implementation of equipment, assistance with total quality management programs, access to databases, and business networking.

A 1991 National Governors' Association study of 42 programs in 28 states found that half of the programs are administered by universities or community colleges and the remainder are administered by state agencies, quasi-public organizations, or private nonprofit organizations. The programs often target for assistance industries with a large concentration in the state. Although the majority of the programs serve existing manufacturing operations, they sometimes aid small start-up companies.[3]

Most states also have a package of assistance programs designed to nurture start-ups, particularly in high-tech industries. Such programs include small business incubators and a variety of financial assistance instruments such as low-cost loans and loan guarantees, grants, venture capital trust funds, and pooled bond programs. It is difficult to determine exactly how much is being spent by states on programs of this sort since state technology efforts are broad and encompass a range of company sizes. By virtue of the fact that many of these programs nurture start-ups, however, they are nurturing small companies.

The most visible and studied examples of regional concentrations of high-tech companies are Silicon Valley in California and Route 128 in Massachusetts with areas like Austin, Texas, and Research Triangle in North Carolina also receiving considerable attention. The Capital Region of New York State (Albany, Troy and the surrounding communities) is a less developed high-tech region and, therefore, provides a less cluttered example of the range of assets a region can bring to bear and the type of issues an emerging center of technical entrepreneurship faces. Among that region's sources of entrepreneurs and innovations are the following:

[3]M. Clarke, and E. Dobson, *Increasing the Competitiveness of America's Manufacturers. A Review of State Industrial Extension Programs* (Washington, D.C.: National Governors' Association, 1991).

• Rensselaer Polytechnic Institute (RPI), a 170-year-old research university that has graduated 3,120 B.S. engineers, 1,470 M.S. engineers, and 550 Ph.D.'s in science and engineering over the last five years. Further, Rensselaer's School of Management specializes in Technology and Management and offers five-year double degrees in management and science or engineering.

• General Electric Corporate Research Laboratories, a facility employing 1,110 research personnel.

• The State University of New York, Albany, a public university that graduated 1,610 B.S, 455 M.S., and 157 Ph.D.-level scientists during the last five years.

• The Wadsworth Center, a basic research facility of the New York State Department of Public Health, that has spawned a venture firm in the last decade.

• There are over 70,000 college-level students in the region attending more than a half dozen colleges and universities in addition to RPI and SUNY-Albany.

• The region has more than 800 high-tech or manufacturing firms, ranging from a division of General Electric to small entrepreneurial ventures.

Over the course of the last 15 years, the region's community leaders have focused on creating a set of assets to support the start-up and growth of technology-based firms. In 1980 RPI formally established an on-campus incubator facility that provides low-rent space, shared services, and some business assistance to qualified start-up companies. Since its inception, the incubator has spawned more than 90 start-ups, with a high record (greater than 80%) of survival, that currently employ almost 900 people and generate almost $100 million in revenue. The incubator itself is currently being expanded. In 1982 RPI established a technology park, a 1,200-acre real estate development aimed at attracting young technology-based companies, and the technologically intensive operations of larger companies and state agencies. This park now hosts 45 establishments employing more than 1,600 people. While neither the incubator nor the technology park requires a business to have a formal connection to the university, there is a strong predisposition in the behavior of the two enterprises to favor and encourage those businesses that build on, or contribute to, RPI's strengths. A significant attractor for many companies to locate in either the incubator or the technology park is the location of companies in similar stages of development or with similar technical orientations.

In addition to RPI's efforts, both the state of New York, through its Science and Technology Foundation, and the Capital Region's Center for Economic Growth, through its Technology Development Council, offer considerable assistance to technology-based start-ups. For example, the New York State Science and Technology Foundation supports joint university-industry centers for advanced technology at New York universities. These centers are explicitly designed to support the development of industrially relevant technologies with high potential for commercialization. Two such centers are located in the Capital Region, the Center for Advanced Thin Films and Coatings at SUNY-Albany and the Center for Advanced Technology in Automation and Robotics at Rensselaer. The Foundation also operates a Manufacturing Technology Center, supported by federal, state, and private funds, that assists small- and medium-sized companies in adapting new manufacturing technology to their needs. Additionally, the Foundation operates a small venture seed capital fund to invest in New York-based start-ups and a venture/financing referral service to put start-ups in touch with potential investors.

The Capital Region Technology Development Council's is a regional (11-county) economic development agency funded primarily by the state of New York and private funds. While the Technology Development Council offers a range of networking and business services, the flagship service is a business advisory program that enlists experienced technical and business people as volunteers to serve as senior level management consultants (about 300 volunteers) to provide services such as legal, risk assessment, commercialization, and business planning for client companies. Some of these people also invest in the small firms. The aid supplied these firms is often in the form of workshops and networks, as well as individual consultation. The Technology Council also plays an important role in providing information about, and a connection to, resources outside the region. One of the most visibly successful efforts they have undertaken in recent years is to assist companies in the region in applying for federal Small Business Innovative Research grants, more than $5 million in such grants having been won by small, local ventures in 1994.

In short, the Capital Region seems to have much of the basic infrastructure in place to develop as a regional, high-tech entrepreneurial center. The region is succeeding in starting companies, but it now faces new issues in learning to help these firms grow to significant size. Several of these firms have begun to make that transition and must now find skilled business managers willing to take a risk to join a new company; banks familiar with the problems of high-tech, rapid-growth companies and able to evaluate their prospects; and larger equity investors with knowledge of and experience in the region.

The activities in the Capital Region are representative of activities in many regions of the United States that have marshalled their resources to create and develop new businesses and industries. While regional approaches vary—and are necessarily tailored to specific regional assets such as universities and large company research facilities—it is clear that geography matters a great deal. The policies and programs of local, state, and regional governments are important aspects of the local and regional business environment for high-tech companies. The best are responsive to local conditions and reinforce the strengths of the region by promoting technologies and industries of national economic importance.

THE NATIONAL BUSINESS ENVIRONMENT

The opportunity set for small high-tech businesses and start-ups is heavily dependent on industry-specific issues and regional characteristics. There is also, however, an important set of national-scale, and even international, concerns affecting small U.S.-based, technology-driven companies. In many cases, these issues are identical to those affecting the opportunities and performance of larger companies. For example, the first-order impacts of trade barriers, employment laws, government policy on interest rates, international standards, and intellectual property rights fall in similar ways on both larger and small companies, on both technologically sophisticated companies and those with little technical capability or orientation. A number of national policy matters that have been widely recognized as having significant effects on the prosperity and performance of industry generally can have especially profound influences on the viability of small high-tech businesses.

- Maintenance of open and accessible public equity markets. These are key to liquidity for small companies and an important source of capital for growth.
- The tax structure, especially capital gains taxes, which affect the relative attractiveness of longer-term investments such as those necessary to develop new technologies or markets for new products. Lower capital gains taxes (especially for technically risky investments held for longer periods of time) could provide a stimulus for investment in small high-tech companies.
- Regulatory burden on small companies and especially start-ups. It is too easy for well-intentioned regulation from different levels and parts of government to accumulate to the point of crushing a small business or, especially, a start-up.
- Maintenance of a vigorous national portfolio of government-supported and university-based research. Research and related advanced technical education done in a largely nonproprietary setting, in an environment that is favorable for entrepreneurship, are an important national resource for high-tech start-ups.
- The legal environment, especially product liability laws and, for high-tech and high-growth companies, securities fraud liability laws.

The national business environment was not a major focus of this study, but certain aspects of the findings about the role of small business have important implications. For example, a focus on the role of small high-tech companies in pioneering markets and new applications can free them from the burden of expectation that they be the nation's primary job creators; it is much easier to show that important new directions for commercial products and services originated in garages in the Silicon Valley/Stanford nexus than to argue that Intel and Hewlett-Packard are important employers on a national scale. The benefits to consumers of technological advances brought to market by those two companies are large, and would be whether they employ 100,000 people or 50 people.

It is the committee's judgment that the federal government can help maintain the vigor and contribution of small high-tech businesses in the following ways:

- **Working to ensure that financial market regulation, bank-**

ing laws, and securities regulatory agencies are sensitive to the particular demands of small high-tech companies.

• Monitoring, and when possible reducing, the total federal, state, and local regulatory burden on small high-tech companies.

• Maintaining, especially in light of prospective cut-backs in research and development spending, a rich portfolio of university research as a source of potential new commercial opportunities for start-up companies.

UNINTENDED EFFECTS OF GOVERNMENT POLICYMAKING

A wide variety of government actions aimed at and justified by other missions—public safety, environmental quality, and national defense, for example—also have an enormous impact on small technology-intensive companies by affecting the cost of innovation or the risk of failure. For example, in sporting goods and medical devices, suppliers of materials critical for the manufacture of these products have restricted or ceased sales to these sectors to eliminate their exposure to product liability lawsuits. Legislative reforms, in this context, could markedly affect a company's product strategies and posture toward innovation.[4]

Government regulatory actions affect all businesses but they often have a disproportionate effect on small or new companies. These companies may find it more difficult to sustain their businesses under new conditions, financial and otherwise, imposed by regulatory changes. Indeed, part of the risk that small high-tech businesses often shoulder is the risk created by the possibility of unintended consequences of government actions. For this reason, actions that affect the opportunities for such companies—directly or indirectly—should be informed by knowledge of the likely consequences, and those consequences should be weighed against the other, intended consequences of policies and regulations.

It is important to recognize, as well, that the effect of regulation on innovation is not always negative. Government actions regularly create as well as destroy opportunities for small companies.

---

[4]See National Academy of Engineering, *Product Liability and Innovation.* J. Hunziker and T. Jones, eds. (Washington, D.C.: National Academy Press, 1994).

In environmental testing, for example, regulation is responsible for the creation and sustenance of an entirely new set of opportunities for technically oriented new companies. Nonetheless, it is useful to ask whether it may be possible to lessen the negative effects of government actions (and therefore risk) without taking away from the clear benefits of government actions, for example, in health and safety. Several examples may help to make this clear.

Medical Devices: Innovation as an Investment Decision

Technological innovation depends critically on risk taking by entrepreneurial individuals and small companies. This risk—in various forms—links market size and expected growth, and the impact of size and expected growth on innovation, to external sources of financing. This is especially important in the medical device industry, where the economics of innovation—high technological risk and fragmented markets—tend to be unattractive to larger companies.

Recently, radical changes in the regulatory and policy environment for medical devices appear to be increasing this risk. Food and Drug Administration regulation of medical devices requiring increased numbers of trials and evaluation is increasing the expected time to market for new devices as well as the cost of demonstrating these new devices. The basic rationale for these government actions, of course, is not disputed—regulation of the health and safety of medical devices is an objective of government policy.

But it is important to recognize that even as regulation of medical devices is not directly concerned with economic factors, it may have unforeseen (and expensive) consequences for innovation in medical devices, especially by small and new companies. For example, delays weaken incentives to undertake new product introductions for small firms that need to recoup their investments more quickly than large firms. By increasing the risk—and therefore the difficulty of attracting external financing—these regulatory changes draw into question the viability of innovation by small companies for specialized, low-volume medical devices.

Environmental Testing Labs:
Created and Constrained by Environmental Regulation

In contrast to medical devices, the comprehensive set of environmental laws directed at air and water pollution has created enormous opportunities for small and new, technically oriented companies. Demand for environmental testing services in the United States, now between $1.5 billion and $1.6 billion annually, is almost entirely in response to environmental legislation and regulations. Equally, the opportunities for 1,400 to 1,600 companies—virtually all of these small—that provide these services are in large measure determined by the degree to which future legislation and regulations create new markets and a demand for innovations in testing technology and methodology.

Paradoxically, however, a more subtle effect of regulation in this area has been, in many cases, to remove incentives to explore innovative approaches to improving monitoring capabilities for pollutants. The sources of pollution that the government requires be measured or monitored vary enormously. But the imperative to provide legally defensible data precludes experimentation with new techniques or pollution-reducing technological advances. Instead, approved analytical methods are followed so closely that new innovative techniques, which may be developed by innovative firms and are demonstrably superior to current techniques, are not explored.

The objectives of environmental regulation, of course, are not primarily to encourage innovation, but it is possible that innovation in this area would advance these objectives. There is no question that environmental legislation has created enormous demand for pollution control technologies, for example. In addition, the Environmental Protection Agency has been active in recent years—through initiatives such as Superfund Innovative Technology Evaluation, called the SITE program—in attempting to promote a more flexible approach to the use of new technologies and the use of problem-based methods to replace at least some of the rigid, highly prescriptive testing methods now in use. It is not clear that direct regulation is the best approach to encourage the development of new technologies and reduced levels of pollution.

Networks: Evolution of Regulatory Schemes

The astonishing new complexity of communications and information networks, and the speed of their transformation, is driven to a large extent by new technologies. Chief among these new technologies are advances in computers, which enable the digital encoding (and compression) of information, and in photonics, which enable massive increases in network bandwidth using fiber optics. These technological advances create enormous opportunity for network companies to create proprietary network technologies and to realize the opportunities—video-on-demand, games, and data services are examples—that will drive demand in these new networks.

The question is whether regulation will enable small companies to exploit this new competitive environment. In contrast to medical devices or environmental testing services, which are dominated by large numbers of small competitors, regulation in telecommunications has historically focused on economic regulation of a "natural" monopoly, AT&T. Now, new technologies have enabled companies of all sizes to compete for new opportunities in telecommunications by creating software or the physical assets to create services over these new networks.

Consequently, what these opportunities and technologies will look like, and the speed at which this happens, depends to a large extent on changing regulatory structures. The consent decree that broke up the Bell system in 1982 deregulated long-distance services and regulations have relaxed for almost all sectors of communications. Delays in making regulatory decisions may impede opportunities in networks. For example, pressure on their monopolies in the local loop has left the Bell operating companies anxious to compete with cable television providers by sending video over the telephone network. The current regulatory structure in telecommunications is under a great deal of scrutiny. What items should be provided as universal service and at what cost? With respect to content, to what extent will regulations control the content available to consumers?

Given the risk that government policies will have inadvertent negative consequences for small high-tech businesses, it is important that policymakers concerned with economic growth understand the specific roles that entrepreneurial, high-tech companies play in the development of industrial sectors and of the economy. Policies should be based on the premise that maintaining a national portfolio of high-tech entrepreneurial companies is important.

IMPLICATIONS FOR POLICY

The contribution of this study to policy debates is to ask the question, Given the contributions of small technology-oriented companies to the economy, what principles distinguish good policy and programs from bad? The central findings of this study are that small technically oriented companies assume risks that other companies—large and small—will not and that such risk takers play a particularly important role in technically new and small markets. The relevant question for policymakers, therefore, is, What types of policies substantially encourage (reduce the risk of, or increase the likely return on) commercial technical experimentation by small companies and start-ups?

As the industries studied in this project show, the federal government is—either purposefully or inadvertently—an important force in many industries that depend for their development on small high-tech companies. With regard to purposeful support, government programs that share technological risk by supporting R&D can alleviate some new and small market risks. Also, actions that ensure financing alternatives or facilitate linkages with individuals or institutions that can provide assistance and advice to nascent companies are also important. Government programs like TRP, ATP, and SBIR, are created with the best of intentions and bridge gaps not addressed by private-sector financing for higher-risk ventures. But much ambivalence about these programs remains, as evidenced by talk of cutbacks in funding for the ATP and TRP. The SBIR program was both widely praised and widely criticized during the industry workshops held as part of this study. Praise centered on the fact that funds are available from a number of agencies for exploratory technological work and on the examples of companies successfully founded with SBIR funds. Criticism focused on the way the program has created "SBIR houses" (i.e., companies whose only revenues are from SBIRs and never from products) and is too rigidly oriented on the mission of the agency providing funding. The comments in the workshops mirror the results of a recent General Accounting Office report that reviewed the SBIR program.[5] That report concluded that the quality of submitted and funded proposals remains high but that duplicate funding—companies receiving funding for the same proposals twice, three times, and even five times—has become a problem.

Participants in several of the industry-specific workshops, software and medical devices in particular, noted that programs such as TRP, ATP, and SBIR that could provide financing for small high-tech companies were less useful because of the long review cycles and time delays inherent in highly bureaucratic programs.

With regard to the inadvertent impact of government actions, it is clear that government itself is a substantial source of risk for some small companies; part of the risk that small high-tech businesses often shoulder is the risk created by the unintended consequences of government actions. In the committee's judgment, the consequences of government actions for technically oriented start-ups and small companies—and by implication for their ability to bear technological risk and drive innovation—are often poorly understood both by the public and by policymakers. State and federal actions aimed at, and justified by, other missions—public safety, environmental quality, antitrust, commercial standard setting, and national defense, for example—often have the most profound impact on the opportunities for small high-tech companies. Federal and state actions such as these regularly both create and destroy opportunities for small high-tech businesses.

Given the extreme budget consciousness that appears to pervade Congress, the committee suggests that federal activism on behalf of small business and technology initiatives focus first on establishing mechanisms within government—many of them off-budget—that can improve the general environment for innovative enterprises. Because the structure and implementation of regulations affect the character and speed of innovation (through the risks they can create or remove for companies), regulatory approaches across a wide variety of government functions need to be carefully considered with regard to their impact on small high-tech companies.

---

[5]General Accounting Office, *Federal Research: Interim Report on the Small Business Innovation Research Program*, March 1995.

With regard to programs for active support of small technically oriented businesses, the committee suggests that the central issue is whether federal support will make a difference in the economy's technological development. Private investment is likely to be much greater than any imaginable level of public investment in fragmented, technically dynamic industries with low barriers to entry and a history of (or widely perceived prospect of) successful entrepreneurship. In such industries the important question is, How can government research, development, and demonstration complement the huge private investment (risk taking) to the benefit of the national economy? The challenge in program design and implementation is to articulate and adhere to an industry-specific rationale for government support in light of substantial private-sector activity:

• What is the evidence that market capital is not available to this industry? What leads policymakers to believe that public funds are necessary to drive commercially important technical advance in this industry?

• Is development in this industry amenable to the kind of dynamic, iterative, failure-ridden process that characterizes the most rapidly developing technologies and industries?

• If so, how can a government program constructively seed or accelerate such a process?

Finally, in the committee's judgment, many government policy mechanisms to promote economic growth—some types of federal R&D funding, technical assistance programs, local incubators, university-industry collaborative ventures—need to be designed and managed regionally or locally. Local and regional programs may have an advantage in that they are closer to the resources that small companies need and are potentially more able to adapt to the needs of small high-tech companies.

Appendix

What We Know About
Small Business in America

Small business is an important segment of the U.S. economy, and as such it has merited substantial critical study. The purpose of this section is not to provide the definitive statement on small business in the United States, but rather to summarize some of what is known about small business and thereby put into context this report's discussion of small high-tech companies.

DEFINITIONS

What is a small business? There are numerous measures that could be used to capture the universe of companies defined as "small," including number of employees, business receipts, or the value of assets. However, the most common measure is number of employees. Here, the cutoff used by both the Small Business Administration and the Organization for Economic Cooperation and Development is 100 employees or fewer, although the SBA recognizes that in some industries dominated by a few large players, for example, the automobile or aerospace industries, a company of up to 500 employees would still be considered small.[1]

---

[1]U.S. Small Business Administration, *The State of Small Business: A Report of the President*, (Washington, D.C.: U.S. Government Printing Office, 1992) Page 20.

Another problem in definitions comes up in distinguishing between enterprises (firms, businesses) and establishments (branches, places of business). The SBA notes that small business accounts for 99 percent of all establishments operating in the United States. Further:

> An establishment is defined as any single physical location where business is conducted. An enterprise is a business organization consisting of one or more establishments under the same ownership or control. Most small businesses consist of a single establishment. However, a large firm may own many small establishments; these establishments should not be confused with small firms.[2]

These distinctions are particularly relevant when discussing franchises or subsidiaries. A single franchise, for example, an automobile dealership, owned by an individual would be considered a small business, but multiple franchises with one owner or multiple outlets owned by the parent franchisor would not.

Finally, it is important to note that more than half of all businesses have no employees other than the owner, and many owners work only part-time at their businesses.[3] Using tax return data, which capture all reported business activity, will give a much higher estimate of the number of small businesses than using unemployment insurance data, which exclude millions of part-time, hobby businesses (21.3 million and 5.5 million, respectively).

THE JOB CREATION DEBATE

Since the 1980s, conventional wisdom has held that small firms create most new jobs: a commonly cited figure is that small business creates 80 percent of the new jobs in the United States. This thesis, promoted initially by research analyst David Birch and then adopted by others who found it an excellent vehicle for promoting government programs that favor small business, has come under increasing scrutiny in recent years. Researchers and economists skeptical of this claim have criticized the research methodology

---

[2]Ibid., page 20.
[3]Ibid., page 21.

and interpretations of data and offered alternative explanations for the growing importance of small firms in the United States.[4]

Charles Brown, James Hamilton, and James Medoff, in their book *Employers Large and Small*[5] contend that

- New firms, which tend to be small at birth, generate new jobs when they grow; however, those firms are not necessarily becoming more important sources of employment than large firms.
- Small establishments owned by large firms play an important role in generating jobs.
- The growth of small business industries is more impressive than the job generation of small businesses.
- Small business accounts disproportionately for the two most important components of employment change—the births and deaths of businesses. Existing firms, especially small ones, are on average shrinking, but many new firms enter each year to offset that decline.
- Small business' share of employment has remained relatively unchanged since 1958—about 35 percent of employment is in firms with fewer than 100 employees, and about 50 percent of employment is in firms with fewer than 500 employees.
- Small firms have higher job-loss rates (jobs lost as a result of contractions or closings as a proportion of all employment).

INNOVATION IN SMALL COMPANIES

Another area of debate has focused on whether most innovations originate from large corporate labs or small companies. Zoltan J. Acs and David B. Audretsch in their work on this issue concluded that the question of big vs. small was an oversimplification that did not capture the rich configurations of research efforts

---

[4]See C. Brown, J. Hamilton, and J. Medoff, *Employers Large and Small* (Cambridge, Mass.: Harvard University Press, 1990). S. Davis, J. Haltiwanger, and S. Schuh, *Small Business and Job Creation: Dissecting the Myth and Reassessing the Facts*. Working Paper No. 4492. (Cambridge, Mass.: National Bureau of Economic Research, 1993). B. Harrison, *Lean and Mean: The Changing Landscape of Corporate Power in the Age of Flexibility* (New York: Basic Books, 1994).

[5]C. Brown, J. Hamilton, and J. Medoff, *Employers Large and Small* (Cambridge, Mass.: Harvard University Press, 1990).

and sources of innovation in the United States.[6] Although Bennett Harrison, in his book *Lean and Mean: The Changing Landscape of Corporate Power in the Age of Flexibility* criticizes their methodology, it is worthwhile to note one of their conclusions, namely that industries dominated by large companies, for example, aircraft and automobiles, tend to be more innovative, but it is the small companies in those industries that were likely to produce the innovations.[7]

John Case, an editor at *Inc.* magazine, has pointed out several reasons why this may be so. First, innovative entrepreneurs often have spent some time at big companies before leaving to launch their own firms. Small companies often commercialize technologies developed in corporate R&D labs. Finally, big companies often help small companies bring their products to market, through investing in the companies, providing a distribution system, or assisting in marketing.[8]

A 1992 study funded by the SBA looked at R&D within small firms in four industry groups: office and computing machines, electronic components and accessories, machine tools, and aircraft and parts.[9] It found that small firms in those industries with university research relationships earned more per R&D dollar than large firms. The estimated rates of return on R&D dollars spent were 30 percent for large firms and 44 percent for small firms.

OTHER AREAS OF COMPARISON BETWEEN LARGE AND SMALL FIRMS

A useful comparison of large and small companies is the book noted above by Brown, Hamilton, and Medoff, *Employers Large and Small* (1990). The authors compare small and large firms in such

---

[6]Zoltan J. Acs and David B. Audretsch, *Innovation in Large and Small Firms: An Empirical Analysis* (Vol. 78, No. 4. September 1988. Pp. 678-690).

[7]B. Harrison, *Lean and Mean. The Changing Landscape of Corporate Power in the Age of Flexibility* (New York: Basic Books, 1994)

[8]John Case, "Sources of Innovation," *Inc.* June (1989): 29.

[9]Albert N. Link and John Rees, *Firm Size and External Research Relationships*, Research Summary Number 129 (U.S. Small Business Administration, Office of Advocacy, December 1992).

areas as wages, benefits, job security, training, unionization, political resources, influence, and intangibles (e.g., proximity to owner-founder).

Wages

Workers in big companies or locations earn more—over 30 percent more—than their counterparts in small firms. Even when other factors such as differences in worker education and experience, differences between manufacturing and service industries, differences in working conditions or union rates, or union avoidance strategies are taken into account, the size-wage premium remains at 10-15 percent.

Benefits

Small firms do not offer many of the fringe benefits, or equivalent benefits in the fringes that are offered, which are available from larger firms. For example, 100 percent of the large firms surveyed for a 1986 SBA study offered health insurance whereas only 55 percent of the firms with fewer than 500 employees offered health insurance. A 1984 Harris survey found that workers' satisfaction with benefits grows with firm size. Differences in fringe benefit offerings can be explained by larger firms' attempts to secure and retain needed labor, the desire to forestall unionization, and lower costs for large firms to set up and run a benefit program.

Job Security

Although much has been written about job loss due to the restructuring of big business, employees in large organizations are actually less likely to be laid off than employees in small companies. Data collected on the U.S. manufacturing sector for the period 1950-1971 showed that a smaller proportion of the workforce was likely to be laid off each month in large establishments than in small establishments. Another study conducted in 1980 and 1981 found that even though large employers are more likely to be in high-layoff industries, within an industry, large employers offer more job security.

Training

It is commonly thought that because many workers start out in small firms, they are acquiring their training in those firms as well. However, results of studies on training and firm size are mixed. One study found that new employees received far more hours of both formal and informal training in establishments with more than 500 workers than in smaller workplaces. This can be attributed to the fact that large firms can train more people in one class with a single instructor and there is more extensive informal training by coworkers. A later study showed the smallest and largest establishments providing the most training.

Unionization

Eighteen percent of the U.S. workforce is unionized, and workers in large companies are much more likely than those in small ones to be unionized. Even though the data on unionization rates and firm size imply that union representation must be more desirable to workers in large firms than small ones, a Harris survey for the AFL-CIO found that workers of small employers were much more likely to vote for unionization than were the workers of large employers. The discrepancy may reflect the fact that unions gain more from organizing larger units and that larger (and by implication longer-lived) employers have been exposed longer to the possibility of being unionized.

Political Resources

Small business is viewed by the public as having little influence in politics. This can be attributed in part to its association in the public's mind with mom-and-pop stores or the lone entrepreneur. Also, there is no single lobbying organization for small business to project a unified message for that sector of the economy. However, it is important to note the political clout of trade groups and professional associations representing the interests of individual industries that are composed primarily of small businesses. Of the top 10 contributors to political action committees (PACs) in 1986, five represented small business constituencies: realtors, home builders, physicians, trial lawyers, and insurers. A Federal Election Commission study found that small-business PACs contributed nearly two-thirds as much as big-business PACs to Senate and House candidates and roughly the same amount as PACs associated with labor. In a survey of trade associations, small-business associations had approximately 20,000 staff, compared with 15,000 for big-business associations and 4,000 for labor unions. Small business also represents a sizable voting block in every congressional district. The positive public image of small business is also an asset; the public is much more likely to support programs endorsed by small-business advocates than programs endorsed by labor or big-business groups. Journalists also rate the credibility of small business much higher than that of big business or labor.

Influence

A number of studies of roll-call votes have pointed out that small-business PAC money does indeed sway votes. Actual influence may be greater, however, considering the fact that small-business PAC contributions may affect the outcome of elections so that candidates that favor their positions are more likely to end up in Congress. Another measure of small-business influence is that small and large firms are not subject to the same regulatory compliance and reporting requirements. Studies have shown that when subject to health and safety regulations, enforcement tends to be more lax in small firms so that the workers are less protected than their counterparts in larger firms.

Intangibles

Small companies are said to offer "intangibles" that large firms do not. These include proximity to, and guidance of, an owner-founder, potential to move up quickly if the firm grows quickly, opportunities for an equity interest, and the opportunity to get involved in more aspects of a company's business. However, using quit rates among workers with the same wages as a gauge of employee satisfaction, it has been found that workers in large firms have a much lower quit rate than their counterparts in small ones. Although there is more internal job movement among workers of large employers, even for workers for whom internal job movement was not an issue, those working for large employers were less likely to change their employer. Large firms also appear to have longer queues of qualified job applicants for the positions they offer.

THE DATA ON SMALL HIGH-TECH COMPANIES

The Office of Science and Technology Policy estimates that there are 75,000 small high-tech firms in the United States with approximately 1.75 million to 2 million direct employees engaged in key high-technology areas. SBA studies note that small high-tech firms create twice their proportional share of new jobs, that they produce two to four times the number of products and patents per R&D dollar, and generate half of all major technical innovations leading to commercial patented products.[10]

The National Science Board's 1993 *Science and Engineering Indicators* notes that, "many of the new technologies and industries seen as critical to the Nation's future economic growth are closely identified with small business."[11] These technology fields include automation, biotechnology, computer hardware, advanced materials, photonics and optics, software, electronic components, and telecommunications.

Even though the late 1980s saw a sharp decline in company formation from the earlier part of the decade, almost half of all U.S. high-tech companies operating in 1993 were formed since 1980.[12] Sixty percent of companies in computer-related and bio-technology fields were formed since 1980. Software companies account for the greatest number of small business start-ups among all technology fields; 34 percent of the 10,000 new high-tech companies formed since 1980 and in existence in 1993 were software development or servicing businesses (See Figure 1 and Table 2).

---

[10]*The State of Small Business: A Report of the President* (U.S. Small Business Administration, 1990, and Cognetics Consultants, Inc. 1991). See also William K. Scheirer, *Small Firms and Federal R&D* (Office of Management and Budget, 1977) and *Innovation in Small Firms*, Issue Alert Number 8 (U.S. Small Business Administration, July 1986).

[11]*Science and Engineering Indicators—1993* (U.S. National Science Board, 1994, p. 185).

[12]Ibid.

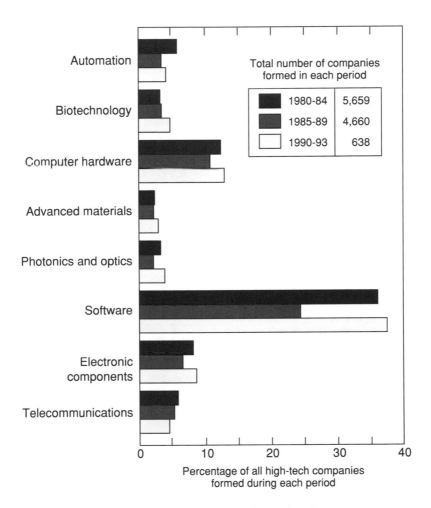

FIGURE 1   High-tech business formation, by technology.
Note: Data reflect information collected through July 1993. Reprinted from Science & Engineering Indicators—1993 (National Science Board, 1994).

TABLE 2 High-tech companies formed in the United States: 1980-93

Period formed	All high-tech fields	Automation	Biotechnology	Computer hardware	Advanced materials	Photonics & optics	Software	Electronic components	Telecom-munications	Other fields[1]
Total, all years	22,728	1,534	558	2,176	869	823	5,644	2,611	1,267	7,246
				Number of companies						
1980-93	10,957	490	358	1,253	243	296	3,395	807	593	3,522
1980-84	5,659	315	178	683	137	171	2,026	453	324	1,372
1985-89	4,660	150	150	489	88	100	1,131	299	239	2,014
1990-93	638	25	30	81	18	25	238	55	30	136
				Percentage of all high-tech companies formed during each period						
Total, all years	100.0	6.7	2.5	9.6	3.8	3.6	24.8	11.5	5.6	31.9
1980-93	100.0	4.5	3.3	11.4	2.2	2.7	31.0	7.4	5.4	32.1
1980-84	100.0	5.6	3.1	12.1	2.4	3.0	35.8	8.0	5.7	24.2
1985-89	100.0	3.2	3.2	10.5	1.9	2.1	24.3	6.4	5.1	43.2
1990-93	100.0	3.9	4.7	12.7	2.8	3.9	37.3	8.6	4.7	21.3
				Percentage of total U.S. high-tech companies, by field						
Total, all years	100.0	100.0	100.0	100.0	100.0	100.0	100.0	100.0	100.0	100.0
1980-93	48.2	31.9	64.2	57.6	28.0	36.0	60.2	30.9	46.8	48.6
1980-84	24.9	20.5	31.9	31.4	15.8	20.8	35.9	17.3	25.6	18.9
1985-89	20.5	9.8	26.9	22.5	10.1	12.2	20.0	11.5	18.9	27.8
1990-93	2.8	1.6	5.4	3.7	2.1	3.0	4.2	2.1	2.4	1.9

NOTE: Data reflect information collected on new high-tech companies formed through June 1993.

[1]Other fields are chemicals, defense-related, energy, environmental, manufacturing equipment, medical, pharmaceuticals, subassemblies and components, test and measurement, and transportation.

SOURCE: CorpTech database Rev. 8.2 (Wellesley Hills, MA: Corporate Technology Information Services, Inc.), special tabulations.

Reprinted from *Science & Engineering Indicators - 1993* (National Science Board, 1994).

Biographies of Committee Members

Henry Kressel (Chairman) is currently a managing director of Warburg, Pincus & Co. Dr. Kressel has occupied various positions at the RCA Laboratories including Vice President for Research and Development, with responsibilities for power devices, integrated circuits, lasers, and other optoelectronic devices and systems. A graduate of Yeshiva College in physics, Dr. Kressel received an M.S. degree in applied physics from Harvard University, an M.B.A. from the Wharton School, and a Ph.D. in materials sciences from the University of Pennsylvania. Dr. Kressel is a member of the National Academy of Engineering.

Elwyn R. Berlekamp is Professor of Mathematics and of Electrical Engineering/Computer Science at UC Berkeley. Dr. Berlekamp also founded and until recently served as president of Cyclotomics, now part of Eastman Kodak. At Cyclotomics Dr. Berlekamp led the development of a variety of electronic architectures and integrated circuits to implement advanced algorithms for encoding and decoding that are now widely used in aerospace and commercial applications. Dr. Berlekamp received his B.S., M.S., and Ph.D. degrees in electrical engineering from the Massachusetts Institute of Technology, and is a member of the National Academy of Engineering.

H. Kent Bowen is Professor of Technology and Operations Management at the Harvard Business School. Previously, he was Ford Professor of Engineering at the Massachusetts Institute of Technology. As co-director of MIT's Leaders for Manufacturing Program, he guided a research and education program developing the fundamentals for "big-M" manufacturing. His past research included studies of advanced materials and materials processing. He received his B.S. degree in ceramic engineering from the University of Utah and his Ph.D. degree from MIT. Dr. Bowen is a member of the National Academy of Engineering.

Ruth M. Davis is president and CEO of the Pymatuning Group, Inc., which specializes in modernization strategies and technology development for industry. She is also chairman of the Aerospace Corporation. Previously, she was Assistant Secretary of Energy for Resource Applications, and Deputy Under Secretary of Defense for Research and Advanced Technology. Dr. Davis received her B.A. from American University, and her M.A. and Ph.D. degrees from the University of Maryland, all in mathematics. Dr. Davis is a member of the National Academy of Engineering.

Joseph F. Engelberger is founder and formerly president of Unimation Inc. Dr. Engelberger is widely recognized as the "Father of Robotics," and has been a driving influence in the creation of the industrial robotics industry. Currently Dr. Engelberger is the Chairman of Transitions Research Corporation, which aims to improve the spectrum of sensory perception of robots to enable mobile, sensate robots for the service sector. He received his B.A. and M.A. degrees from Columbia University, and is a member of the National Academy of Engineering.

Gerald D. Laubach is formerly president of Pfizer, Inc., and has served as chair of the Pharmaceutical Manufacturers Association. Dr. Laubach is a research chemist by training, and started as a laboratory scientist at Pfizer. He received a B.A. from the University of Pennsylvania and a Ph.D. in organic chemistry from the Massachusetts Institute of Technology. Dr. Laubach is a member of the National Academy of Engineering and the Institute of Medicine and chaired the IOM Committee on Technological Innovation in Medicine.

Robert A. Pritzker is president and CEO of The Marmon Group, Inc. Mr. Pritzker is also a director of Hyatt Corporation. Mr. Pritzker's entire professional life has been in industrial management, and he holds executive positions in the Marmon Group's more than 60 autonomous companies worldwide. He received a B.S. degree in industrial engineering from the Illinois Institute of Technology, and lectures at several schools on business management. Mr. Pritzker is a member of the National Academy of Engineering.

Roland W. Schmitt is president emeritus of Rensselaer Polytechnic Institute, and president from 1988 to 1993. Before becoming president of Rensselaer, he served as senior vice president of science and technology for GE and as a member of GE's Corporate Executive Council. He is also a member and former chairman of the National Science Board, the policy group for the National Science Foundation. Dr. Schmitt received his undergraduate and Master's degrees in mathematics and physics from the University of Texas, and his Ph.D. in physics from Rice University. Dr. Schmitt is a member of the National Academy of Engineering.

George L. Turin has been chairman of Electrical Engineering and Computer Science at UC Berkeley, and Dean of Engineering and Applied Sciences at UCLA. He retired as vice president of technology at Teknekron Corporation, a consortium of high-technology companies of which he is a co-founder. Dr. Turin received his B.S., M.S., and Ph.D. degrees in electrical engineering, all from the Massachusetts Institute of Technology. Dr. Turin is a member of the National Academy of Engineering.